BEYOND THE

AN EXPLORATION OF NEWCASTLE'S CHURCHES,

CHURCHYARDS, CEMETERIES AND BURIAL GROUNDS

St Nicholas' Church, view from the south, 1715.

ALAN MORGAN

TYNE BRIDGE PUBLISHING

The author's grateful thanks to: Bill Atkinson, Jo Bath, Norman Burn, Hilary Clixby, Ron Coulson, Michael Cullen, Jimmy Donald, Steve Ellwood, Robin Gard, James Gibson, Elspeth Gould, Olive Graham, Tony Henderson, John Nolan, Barry Redfern, Phil Thirkell, John Williams. Thanks also to Local Studies at Newcastle City Library; Tyne Bridge Publishing; Newcastle Bereavement Services; Cemetery staff: Dave Conway, Malcolm Watson, Mark.

Modern photography by Alan Morgan unless otherwise indicated; other illustrations are from the collections of Newcastle City Library, unless otherwise indicated.

Also by Alan Morgan: *A Fine and Private Place: Jesmond Old Cemetery*; *Bygone Jesmond Dene*; *Bygone Jesmond Vale*; *Bygone Lower Ouseburn*; *Bygone Sandyford and Cradlewell*; *Bygone Shieldfield*, Tyne Bridge Publishing.

Front cover: St Andrew's Cemetery; back cover: St Andrew's Churchyard.

For those intending to visit cemeteries in Newcastle opening times are:

October and March		April - September	
Mon -Fri	8.00am - 5.45pm	*Mon-Fri*	8.00am - 6.45pm
Sat, Sun	10.00am - 4.45pm	*Sat, Sun, Bank Holidays*	10.00am - 4.45pm

November - February

Mon -Thur	8.00am - 3.45pm	On public holidays, Mother's Day, Father's Day and Remembrance Sunday Cemeteries will open at 10.00 am.
Fri	8.00 am - 2.45pm	
Sat, Sun	10.00am - 3.45pm	For further information: www.newcastle.gov.uk

Supported by Strettle of Newcastle Ltd.
incorporating:
Strettle Memorials, Strettle Funeral Services
and Strettle Fireplaces

'Serving the needs of the bereaved in the North East of England for almost 60 years'.

About Strettle of Newcastle Ltd. ...
Established in 1946, with its head office and workshops still on the original site at Shiremoor in North Tyneside, the name Strettle has become synonymous with cemeteries and churchyards and the art of commemoration in stone. This independent family owned company carries out monumental masonry, funeral arrangements and specialist fireplace installations throughout the region.

ISBN: 1857951026

Published by: City of Newcastle upon Tyne, Education & Libraries Directorate, Newcastle Libraries & Information Service, Tyne Bridge Publishing, 2004   **www.tynebridgepublishing.co.uk**

Printed by Elanders Hindson, North Tyneside

Contents

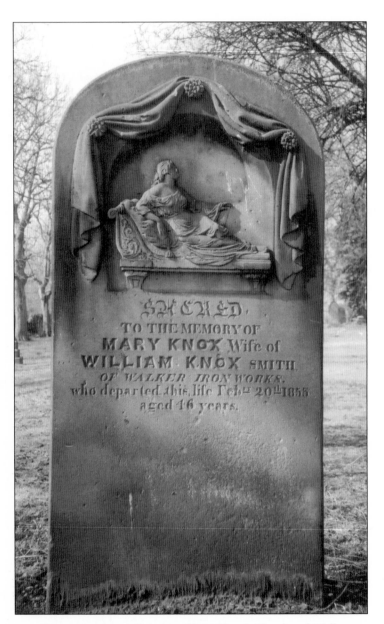

Every gravestone tells a story. Christ Church Churchyard, Walker.

BY THIS MAY I REMEMBERED BE ...

When I am dead and laid in grave
And all my bones are rotten,
By this may I remembered be
When I should be forgotten.

(from a sampler, 1736)

The seemingly popular book *A Fine and Private Place: Jesmond Old Cemetery*, focused on the remarkable story of that 'Highgate of the North', Jesmond Old Cemetery, the people buried there, the funeral practices of Newcastle's prosperous Victorian middle-classes whose territory it was, and the cemetery's history since its opening in 1836.

The fascinating story of the other burial places in the city still needs to be told – the parish churches and churchyards that accommodated Newcastle's citizens from before the middle ages until the mid-19th century; the municipal cemeteries that were created because of overcrowding and a crisis in public health; the private burial grounds of non-conformists and religions other than the established Church of England. I have visited all of the accessible ones, and investigated the memorials of their many and various occupants.

Beyond the Grave explores many of the known burial sites in Newcastle and its suburbs. Some are still active, others are closed and the rest long-vanished. As well as identifying the burial sites of the famous – and not so famous – and giving a brief description of their lives, the book contains plans of the larger cemeteries to help readers who wish to visit the places described. A brief look is also taken at the history of burial practices through the ages, the sometimes elaborate memorials that have been erected for the departed, and at the terrifying epidemics that have swept Newcastle over the centuries.

FROM THE EARLIEST DAYS

People have been living and dying in the Newcastle area for thousands of years, and many of them are still here beneath our feet. In Newcastle, a few Bronze Age burials, dating from c2000-c1200BC, have been found. During the early Bronze Age the usual method of burial was in small, shallow stone-lined graves known as cists. They usually contained a crouched body or ashes in an urn, often with a food vessel and sometimes personal possessions. The cist was covered with a large flat stone, and protected by a distinctive circular mound of earth or stone. Many corpses were buried in ditches or pits, others were simply left to decompose. Wooden coffins were extremely rare at this period.

The late Romans sometimes buried their dead in stone coffins. A law forbidding burials within Roman settlements meant that graves usually lined the roads leading out of town. A 19th century excavation revealed two Roman stone coffins close to Newcastle's Castle Keep, on a site which was probably just outside the Roman settlement of Pons Aelius. The Keep is built on the site of another burial ground – a Saxon cemetery, used from about 700AD and containing over 660 bodies (see page 168).

Christian churches, though few in number, began to make an appearance from the late Roman period in the 4th and 5th centuries AD. Wayside crosses, which were tall enough to attract the attention of passers by, were used as the main focus for worship, but gradually Christians started to make use of timber, wattle and daub buildings or structures adapted from other purposes to hold their services. There are many examples of early churches built from reclaimed Roman stone. Stone-built churches became the norm after the Norman conquest.

LOCATION, LOCATION, LOCATION

Burial within the church itself gave the opportunity to lie closer to God in death. Many of those who wrote wills requested a particular burial place. Initially burial inside churches was reserved for saints, bishops and royalty, but over time it was possible for anyone with a decent reputation and sufficient funds to get a space inside the church and it was unusual for a gentleman to be anywhere else. A well-appointed spot within a church was much sought after and the closer you were buried to the altar the better. As well as the spiritual benefit, it

One Devonshire epitaph nicely demonstrates the importance of wealth in positioning within the church:

Here lie I at the chapel door
Here lie I because I'm poor
The further in the more you'll pay
Here lie I as warm as they.

gave status to surviving family members and provided security for the corpse. People were expected to leave land or money to the church for this privilege.

Some noble families, especially in the 17th century, went one stage further and had a vault constructed under the church. Some were simply brick-lined spaces with room for only a couple of coffins, others were deep shafts in which coffins could be placed one on top of the other, separated by iron bars. Other vaults were cavernous chambers, big enough for several interments. Some churches also had communal vaults. All this led to overcrowding, and instability in the foundations of churches. When Samuel Pepys was organising his brother's burial in a London church in 1664, the gravedigger was prepared to 'justle' the bodies already in the chosen space in the middle aisle for sixpence.

GOD'S ACRE: THE PARISH CHURCHYARD

The parish churchyard was the last resting place for most people. Churchyards were established from the late 6th century to remind churchgoers to include the dead in their prayers. By the 10th century, the size of a churchyard was set at around one acre, (4,840 square yards) hence the expression 'God's acre'; 'acre' means 'field' in Old English.

In the medieval period this resting place was only temporary for most people. As the churchyard filled up, the bones of all but the richest were moved and stored in a charnel house or bone store so the land could be re-used for more burials. At this time most people were buried in a shallow grave, dressed only in a shroud (often a large sheet, wound round the body and tied at the head and feet) and brought to the unmarked grave on a plank of wood. An act of 1580 stated that 'any person found making a coffin except for a person of rank shall be fined ten shillings'. About this time the 'parish coffin' was introduced to bring corpses for burial. Once the body was transferred to the grave, the coffin was rinsed out with vinegar to await the next temporary occupant. After the great plague of 1665, this practice was, understandably, discontinued and the profession of undertaking began.

Until the 17th century churchyards were largely free of permanent memorials and were used for all kinds of activities including sports, fairs, markets, the grazing of animals and archery practice. They were also used as sanctuaries in time of war, although if blood was shed in a fight, the churchyard would be closed until it could be purified with prayers and the sprinkling of holy water.

Over time, a growing desire emerged for a more permanent resting place. The location of graves became important. Certain areas were seen as better than others and extra money might buy a space where another coffin would not be put on top of yours. Well-off families favoured the south side of the chancel, while others, including clerics, often preferred to be buried near the east window. The smaller northern side of the churchyard, where the sun does not shine, was seen as the haunt of the devil. At one time it was left unconsecrated and used for the burial of the unbaptised, the excommunicated, suicides, criminals, strangers and paupers. Victims of epidemics were often buried here in unmarked communal pits. However, there was less chance of disturbance here: 'And that I might longer undisturb'd abide, I choos'd to be laid on the northern side' (1807 epitaph from Lincolnshire).

As it became easier and cheaper to transport stone, permanent memorials became more popular. Many families reserved plots, sometimes putting up a stone before any member died, to confirm their rights to the ground, and guarantee against a hard-up or forgetful heir.

An Act of Parliament enforced burial in woollen shrouds between 1667 and 1814. This was intended to boost the wool trade and discourage the use of linen. Heavy fines of £5 were levied on anyone who broke the law – which the wealthy usually did!

MONUMENTS AND MEMORIALS

INDOORS ...

Until the 11th century, graves, even those of royalty, went unmarked. However, from the 12th century, cross slabs appeared in church floors over the burial sites of important people. They rarely had written inscriptions, but often provide other clues to the deceased's identity. As well as a cross they could bear a sword for a man, a pair of shears for a spinster, keys for a married woman, and a chalice if the grave's occupant was a priest. The shears and book on the illustrated slab may indicate a prioress of the nearby Nunnery. Often the tools of the deceased's trade were also depicted. Some cross slabs are preserved in Newcastle's parish churches and museums.

Cross slabs developed into ledger stones, which were sometimes decorated with engraved plates known as brasses. They can give valuable information about the costume, armour and heraldry of the period.

A fine 13th century medieval cross slab with shears and book in St Nicholas' Cathedral.

From the 13th century, tomb chests started to appear. Made from local stone, the sides were often decorated with carvings and an effigy of the deceased lying on the top. From the 14th century tomb chests were often covered by stone canopies. Fashions changed in the 16th century, with Roman-style detail (columns, arches and pediments) replacing gothic designs on monuments. There was also a new trend for mural memorials – tablets set into the church wall. By the 17th century tomb chests were largely superseded by monuments in the classical or Roman style, with urns, drapes, flowers and leaves. Expensive imported marble was beginning to replace local stone. Church burials were officially forbidden at the Reformation, but many still took place as long as a cash incentive was offered to church authorities. They were finally discontinued after the Act of Parliament of 1854 forbidding urban burials.

AND OUT

From the mid-17th century, churchyards began to be filled with permanent memorials. Headstones were probably a Roman invention. At first they were small, thick, crudely cut stones, often with matching footstones. Later the stones grew in size. Often both sides were used for inscriptions. Ledger stones were large, flat, rectangular stones which covered graves. Although they acted as a deterrent to grave robbers they were prone to wear and weathering. There were also more elaborate tombs as the inside of churches became full.

It became fashionable to decorate these stones and tombs with emblems. Skilled masons could carve a range of designs, each with a specific meaning. Until the early 1700s, symbols of mortality were popular. Skulls, bones and corpses in winding sheets or coffins simply represented death. Darts, scythes and bows and arrows reminded passers-by that death was an ever present threat. Hourglasses, candles and sundials represented the swift passage of time. The tools of a sexton (a spade and a turf cutter) represented preparation for death, while snakes and serpents warned against sin. Inverted symbols such as torches, horseshoes and cannons represented a life extinguished.

During most of the 1700s, grave orna-

A 1760 stone from St Nicholas' Churchyard, South Gosforth, with skull, hourglass and bible.

mentation became more optimistic, with symbols representing immortality replacing those of mortality. Angels were messengers of the Resurrection, while a dove represented the Holy Spirit. Wreaths symbolised immortality. Palm fronds and sprays of leaves represented victory over death. Trumpets, and sometimes more complicated scenes of the corpse emerging from its coffin surrounded by angels blowing trumpets, reminded people of Resurrection. A

A now vanished stone from St John's churchyard with a fine selection of emblems – angel with trumpet, skull, and coffin.

winged sun disk symbolised the journey of the soul to the after life, torches represented eternal life and a book, was the Bible the book of life or book of knowledge. A cherub represented the soul leaving the body for heaven.

In the 1700s, wooden grave boards, bedheads or 'leaping' boards (a low wooden rail between two posts) were popular memorials, particularly in areas short of stone. Very few have survived.

In Victorian Britain, fashions changed again. The trend for all things classical had a strong influence, and obelisks, popularised in Rome as a Christian symbol, became favoured as did urns. Their height advantage made them attractive despite their pagan origins and lack of surface area for inscriptions. Partially draped urns represented the Resurrection. Although unpopular for nearly 300 years after the Reformation, crosses began to return. They were often mounted on three steps representing faith, hope and charity. A broken column signified a life cut short or the end of a family line.

A broken column in Elswick Cemetery remembers four young engineers killed on the SS Leopold and SS Thornby, in 1874.

NEWCASTLE BEREAVEMENT SERVICES are, in 2004, testing the gravestones in cemeteries for safety reasons, as part of a national directive. As this process takes place some stones are being laid flat, with the possibility of restitution in the future. Because of this, some cemeteries may not look exactly as shown in the photographs in this book.

FUNERAL CUSTOMS, SUPERSTITIONS AND BELIEFS

For many centuries it was considered extremely important to please the spirit of the deceased. If it became envious of those still living it could return to haunt them. Therefore new clothes and shoes were avoided and complimentary remarks were made about the deceased (remembered today when we say 'don't speak ill of the dead'). Small items of food and clothing were often left in the grave, along with rosemary or evergreens as a token of remembrance. It is also the reason why we still leave flowers at graves.

The restless spirit needed assistance to leave the house as quickly as possible so doors and windows were opened, fires were extinguished to make the house less comfortable, and clocks were stopped to confuse the spirit.

Mourners had to remain inconspicuous to prevent the spirit from becoming harmful. They wore black clothes to help them escape notice, more than to show grief for the deceased. Some widows wore veils to disguise themselves. Pregnant women were advised not to attend funerals. Mirrors were covered and houses and carriages were darkened by drawing curtains or blinds. Animals were removed from the premises and perishable food was thrown away. It was bad luck to leave the corpse unattended – a tradition which led to the development of wakes. Mourners were expected to touch the brow of the deceased – this was because the body of a murdered person was said to bleed at the touch of the murderer, and no one wished to refuse the test. Candles were burned near the corpse and salt was placed on the body. Fire and salt were regarded as antidotes to evil, as was the soil thrown on the coffin during the funeral service. The coffin was carried from the house feet first to make it impossible for the deceased to signal to mourners to accompany him. The church bell tolled, nine times for a man, six for a woman and three for a child, which helped the soul to start its journey to eternity.

Funeral processions were never to halt, so they were given right of way over other traffic. Gates had to be opened in advance. Anyone meeting a funeral procession had to remove his hat and follow the procession for a short way otherwise he, too, would die before long.

To keep the spirit underground stones were placed on top of the grave. These developed into cairns and eventually gravestones. The phrase in the funeral service 'ashes to ashes' derives from the ashes which were placed under the corpse to absorb disease, then deposited in the grave to remove evil spirits.

PLAGUE, PESTILENCE AND CHOLERA

Epidemics, plague and the Black Death were a frequent and unpleasant feature of medieval life in Newcastle and the surrounding area. The earliest recorded visitation was in 1234 when 'a grievous plague' beset Newcastle for three years. During the Black Death of 1348 about one third of England's population fell victim to the disease and an early form of quarantine was introduced when 'only persons on essential journeys were allowed to leave the kingdom'. Famine often followed plague, and it is recorded that in 1438, poor people ate bread made from fern roots to stave off starvation.

During the 16th century outbreaks of the disease were particularly frequent and there are many references to 'the pestiferous and ragious sweat'. The town's account books record payments made for the burial of victims – fivepence was paid to bury Beyell Taytte – but the locations of the burials are not recorded. In 1579 2,000 people (about one fifth of the town's population) died of disease.

In 1589 another visitation claimed the lives of 1,827 people, and for the first time we know the locations of burials: St John's 340, All Saints 400, St Andrew's 400, St Nicholas' 103, Chapel of St Ann's 509, and elsewhere 75.

There were many attempts to contain the infection. During the 1579 outbreak ships were warned not to approach the town. In 1590 Agnes Taylor dictated her will through the window of her house in Denton Chare to the curate of St Nicholas', and the parish clerk of St John's who were afraid to enter the plague-ridden house. In 1597 healthy people (and perhaps some who were already infected) left the town and took refuge at St Ann's chapel, the hospital of St Mary Magdalene at Barras Bridge, and Spital Tongues.

The town was rarely free of major infectious epidemics for more than a few months at a time. There was another outbreak in the autumn of 1603, which carried on throughout most of 1604. A hundred victims were buried in All Saints churchyard, and more plague burials are recorded in the registers of the other parish churches. Despite the disease raging through the town, the Corporation still wanted amusement and paid the considerable sum of four shillings for a tumbler to entertain 'Mr Mayor and his brethren'.

Another outbreak in 1625 saw so many deaths that parish clerks were having difficulty coping. The parish registers at St John's were in a confused state because of the number of deaths, the understandably hasty funerals and the difficulty of obtaining information about the deceased. Smoking a pipe was regarded as some protection against infection.

Over a period of several months in 1636, 5,037 people died in Newcastle. Trade was at a

standstill and the town was so quiet that the streets were covered in grass. That year the town could not afford to pay the 'ship money' due to the King. Burying such a large number of victims must have taken up a considerable amount of space, but we have no idea where the interments took place – it was almost certainly outside the town walls.

The ironically named 'Jolly Rant' raged in Newcastle in 1675, claiming 924 people.

The 'plague' of the 19th century was cholera, which was caused by polluted drinking water. The disease winds its way through the pages of this book. There were outbreaks in 1831-32 when 306 people died out of a population of 53,000; in 1848-49 412 people perished from a population of 80,000; and 1853 which saw 1,533 deaths out of a population of 90,000. Improvements in public health meant the outbreak of 1866 claimed only a few lives.

In 1831-32, 31 cholera victims were buried east of the north transept in St Nicholas' churchyard and 87 in All Saints Churchyard. Eventually, however, Newcastle's churchyards were becoming so crowded that burials were moved away from the town centre to Ballast Hills, St Ann's Chapel and Westgate Hill. In each of the parishes, buildings were allocated to receive the cholera victims. Those living in St Nicholas' parish were sent to the Castle, in All Saints a large house on the North Shore behind Sandgate was used and St John's and St Andrew's parishes used St John's Poor House in Bath Lane.

In infected parts of the town, both house interiors and streets were washed with lime. The Theatre Royal was closed for the winter season, and the annual Christmas Ball and Supper at the Mansion House was postponed. The barracks were closed, soldiers were excluded from the town and all ships were quarantined in port. Precautions regarding funeral arrangements included interment within 12 hours of death; graves at least six feet deep and in a designated part of the burial ground; corpses barred from the church, with funerals taking place at the graveside; quicklime thrown into the graves and special transport provided by the Corporation. Church bells tolled continuously as corpses passed through the streets in rapid succession – many without a single mourner. The person leading the horse pulling the hearse held the bridle as far away from the vehicle as possible to try to avoid infection.

A announcement in the Newcastle Journal for Saturday 1 October 1853 notes the reduction in daily funerals as the cholera epidemic relaxed its grip.

TO MEMBERS OF THE CHURCH OF ENGLAND. THE VICAR OF NEWCASTLE begs to state, the Number of Funerals having (Thanks be to God !) so much diminished, the Clergy will not, as heretofore, attend in Rotation at the various BURIAL GROUNDS during *the Whole of the Day*, but only at such Times as the Friends of the Deceased may appoint with the Incumbents of the respective Parishes.
The Vicarage, Sept. 29, 1853.

NEWCASTLE'S PARISH CHURCHES

Everyone had the legal right to be buried in their parish churchyard, but over-crowding was, by Victorian times, a pressing problem for urban churches. The outbreaks of cholera in the 1850s finally caused the law to be changed in 1854; further burials were forbidden in town parish churches and churchyards and sub-urban cemeteries were created. There had been a movement in England towards private cemeteries from 1819, to provide a secluded and secure resting place amongst those of similar social status for those who could afford the fees. Long before this time, members of other religions, or Christian dissenters who did not wish to have the Anglican burial service, had their own burial grounds.

There are four parish churches in the centre of Newcastle: St Nicholas' (a cathedral from 1882), St John's, St Andrew's and All Saints. They all have associated cemeteries in the sub-urbs. In addition there are several other burial grounds in the city associated with denominations other than the Church of England, and with religions other than Christianity.

In 1825 it was calculated that the total area of Newcastle's four parish churchyards amount-ed to only 2.8 acres. Even in earlier times the allotted acreage was never much more than per-haps twice this. Space was always limited within the town because of the ever expanding pop-ulation within the limits of the 13th century town wall. Most grave spaces would be used many times, and extra soil introduced (often from burials inside the church itself) to increase the capacity of churchyards (which is why churchyards are often higher than the surrounding area). In general, as the town expanded, the churchyards decreased in size.

St Nicholas' Parish Church

A Cathedral from 1882

For several hundred years, up to the late 18th century, the church chancel was the preferred burial place of Newcastle's leading inhabitants, including many of its Mayors, Sheriffs and Aldermen. To be buried as close as possible to the altar was considered 'a passport to paradise' and of course the church welcomed the practice as a valuable source of additional income. Many of these burials were in brick lined vaults.

Additional finance was also raised by creating space for founders' tombs in arched recesses in the south wall of the nave, despite possible weakening of the structure. Most of these recesses are still visible though no tombs remain. Burial on the north side of the nave proved unpopular because heraldic arms in the windows above the tombs never received direct sunlight.

Despite a certain amount of destruction of the church's fixtures and fittings during the Reformation and the Civil War, by 1783 the church interior is reported to have 'afforded a spectacle of extraordinary magnificence'. However, at this time, the four churchwardens decided that a restoration was required, in an attempt to convert the church 'into a kind of cathedral'.

The existing chancel floor, uneven because of centuries of use as a burial ground, was cleared of grave stones, human remains and furniture, then levelled and fitted with new pews. Those monuments and human remains claimed by descendants were then transferred to the nave with a view to continuing the practice of intra mural burials. There were a considerable quantity of unclaimed graves; their monuments were sold as rubble for building foundations (Mosley Street) and human bones were consigned to oblivion in the adjacent charnel house, now used as the crypt.

The lantern tower and steeple of St Nicholas' so impressed Sir Christopher Wren that he represented it in a modified form at St Dunstan's-in-the-East, London.

Grave stones clearly visible on the nave floor, looking towards the western end of St Nicholas', in this 1840s engraving by William Collard.

Wrought iron work, surrounding certain monuments and chapels, realised £4 17s 6d as scrap metal which was then illegally spent by the churchwardens on a feast, but later refunded. It later came to light that the church wardens' books of account had never recorded the sale of the unclaimed monuments many of which were 'large, curious and of blue marble'.

The oldest remaining monument in St Nicholas' Church is the 14th century effigy of a medieval knight (illustrated). Built into a tomb recess in the south transept, it is thought to predate 1325 and probably commemorated a contributor to the early 14th century church-rebuilding programme. Others believe that it relates to Peter le Marechal, once sword bearer to Edward I and later an esquire of Edward II's household, who died in 1322 during border warfare and was buried in St Nicholas' Church. The cross-legged figure, with both feet resting on a lion, is dressed in a long coat of chain mail with surcoat,

sword and shield. The armour plated shoulder protectors (ailettes) are one of only 3 known pairs in England.

WHO'S WHO IN ST NICHOLAS' CATHEDRAL

SARAH BLACKETT (1740-1775) MOTHER-IN-LAW OF ADMIRAL LORD COLLINGWOOD

For over 150 years the Blackett family ruled Newcastle through its aldermen, sheriffs, mayors and MPs, several of whom were buried in the church of St Nicholas' in their family vault. Their funerals were always displays of wealth with much pomp and public ceremony, yet not one of these leading citizens was honoured with a monument other than the usual inscribed flat tombstone. An example of their lavish expenditure occurred at the funeral of Sir Walter Blackett No 2 in 1705, which cost £700, including £127 on 1285 pairs of funeral gloves. Funeral gloves were used as a form of admission ticket to prevent gate crashers.

There is a small wall tablet, dedicated to the memory of the wife of a Blackett, in the south aisle of the chancel. This tablet expresses 'the grief for the loss of an amiable wife from an affectionate husband' and relates to the early death of Sarah Blackett, aged 35 in 1775, wife of John

Lady Collingwood before her marriage in 1791.

Erasmus Blackett, and her burial in St Nicholas' Church. Their only son died as an infant a year later. Their daughter Sarah married Captain Cuthbert Collingwood. Following his victory at Trafalgar and elevation to Admiral Lord Collingwood she became known as Lady Collingwood. Their home still stands in Oldgate, Morpeth. Lady Collingwood died in 1819 and also lies buried in St Nicholas' Church. Her husband received a hero's funeral in 1810 and lies next to Lord Nelson in St Paul's Cathedral, London. A cenotaph to Admiral Collingwood in St Nicholas' is the focus for the annual Trafalgar Day ceremony.

John Erasmus Blackett, a distant relative of the main Newcastle Blackett family, had profitable business interests in coal. He lived his rather short married life in a small but pleasant house in Pilgrim Street (Odeon Cinema site) near the Pilgrim Gate, almost opposite the mansion known as the 'Newe House' belonging to his relative Sir Walter Calverley Blackett. John Erasmus Blackett later moved to a fine new house in Charlotte Square where he died, aged 86 years, in 1814. He too lies buried in St Nicholas' Church. John Erasmus Blackett was four times

Mayor of Newcastle and the last Blackett to hold public office in the town. Blackett Street was named after him.

CAPTAIN JOHN BOVER (1714-1782) NEWCASTLE'S NAVAL RECRUITMENT OFFICER

Captain Bover was Chief of Newcastle's Press Gang for at least 24 years. Despite the fearsome record of the Press Gang, which, before it was abolished in 1833, forcibly 'recruited' men into the navy, Bover appears to have been held in high esteem by 'the leading people in Newcastle'. He had a house in the Bigg Market and was buried with full military honours in St Nicholas. Perhaps significantly, newspaper reports of the funeral added that no keelman, fisherman or merchant seaman were there to pay their respects. A wall tablet exists in the south aisle erected by his only surviving son.

ISAAC COOKSON (1679-1744) FOUNDER OF AN INDUSTRIAL EMPIRE

The Cookson family originated from Settle in Yorkshire, where they had been land owners for a few hundred years. Isaac, the son of a Penrith brazier, arrived in Newcastle in 1704 and successfully ran iron, glass and salt manufacturing businesses, became a coal owner, acquired land and built a spacious mansion. Succeeding generations carried on profitable businesses stimulated by the demand for armaments during the Napoleonic Wars. Hannah, wife of Isaac, followed her husband into this grave 16 years later aged 78. The ledger stone is situated on the south aisle.

MADDISON FAMILY, CORN MERCHANTS AND HOSTMEN

Hostmen were the wealthy 'middle-men' granted a monopoly for the sale of coal and grindstones within the port of Newcastle by Elizabeth I. The Maddisons were a large and successful Newcastle family who are remembered with an elaborate marble monument (illustrated) against the west wall of the south transept, erected around 1635. The Maddison family originated from near Stanhope, Weardale, as corn mer-

chants and later as coal owners. On the left side of the monument is grandfather Lionel (1530-1624) and his wife Jane (kneeling figures). He was Mayor of Newcastle in 1593, 1605 and 1617. In the centre is his son, Henry (1574-1634), who faces his wife Elizabeth kneeling at a prayer desk. He was mayor of Newcastle in 1623. On the right side is grandson Lionel (1595-1646) and his wife Anne (kneeling figures). He was mayor of Newcastle in 1632 and knighted in 1633 by Charles I. A similar monument exists in St George's Chapel to the Hall family (c1635) who were related by marriage to the Maddisons.

Rev. Hugh Moises (1722-1806) Headmaster

Born in Leicestershire, the son of a clergyman, he went to Cambridge University as a classical scholar and was appointed Head (at 27) of Newcastle's then unpopular Grammar School for boys. Improving standards saw his starting salary of £50 a year increased to £120 and he kept his post for 38 years. The site of the school was the former medieval hospital of St Mary the Virgin, Westgate (see page 168). George Stephenson's statue now occupies the site but a nearby gate pillar survives. The school rooms were situated in the hospital's chapel. The headmaster taught in the chancel, his assistants found a space in the nave and the subjects taught included Latin, Greek, Logic, Rhetoric and Divinity.

The Reverend Hugh Moises.

Well known old boys include the Scott brothers, Lord Eldon and Lord Stowell, and Cuthbert Lord Collingwood. King George III was surprised how a naval officer could write so excellent a despatch as Collingwood's account of the battle of Trafalgar. 'But,' added the King, 'I find he was educated by Moises.' Moises died at his Northumberland Street house aged 84 and was buried in St Nicholas. Former pupils subscribed to a white marble wall monument by John Flaxman in the east wall of the south transept. It represents Religion in the form of a woman with her eyes fixed on heaven, leaning on a pillar inscribed with a portrait of the headmaster.

The former medieval hospital of St Mary the Virgin, Westgate.

EDWARD MOSLEY (1717-1798) HOSTMAN

The son of a York apothecary, he was apprenticed to a Newcastle hostman-coal fitter. He was mayor of Newcastle three times (1767, 1774 and 1781) and financed much of the construction costs of Mosley Street. In addition to a ledger stone, a mural monument to his memory exists in the north aisle of the nave.

THE RIDLEY FAMILY: MERCHANT ADVENTURERS, HOSTMEN, LAND OWNERS

Sir Matthew White Ridley (1745-1813).

In 1661, aged 14, Nicholas Ridley travelled from his Bardon Mill home to Newcastle to begin an apprenticeship as a Merchant Adventurer. He had a talent for business and became Sheriff and then Mayor. His grandson Matthew (1712-1778) was a Merchant Adventurer and Hostman, Mayor of Newcastle in 1733, 1751 and 1759, and MP for Newcastle in four successive parliaments. After the death of his first wife he married his wealthy cousin Elizabeth White, heiress of Matthew White's estate at Blagdon, Northumberland. Their 11 children included Sir Matthew White Ridley (1745-1813) who carried on the family business and 'took prompt measures to preserve the town from invasion by repairing the town walls, permanently closing all but three of the town's gates and entrances, and personally financing the provision of guns and ammunition' at the time of the Jacobite Rebellion in 1745. His town house was in Westgate Street (opposite the Assembly Rooms) and his country home was Heaton Hall (now demolished) adjacent to what is now Heaton Park.

Nearly all the Newcastle Ridleys are buried in St Nicholas' Church. Three monuments survive. On the south aisle of the chancel is a marble wall monument to Matthew Ridley (1712-1778) in Roman costume by J. Bacon, regarded as the best monument in the church. On the west wall of the nave is a tall marble monument to commemorate the achievements of Sir Matthew White Ridley (1745-1813). Again the subject is clothed in a Roman toga. John Flaxman was the sculptor. Another marble wall monument on the north side of the great east window commemorates Nicholas Ridley (1750-1805), younger brother of Sir Matthew White Ridley.

FURTHER INTERESTING BURIALS IN ST NICHOLAS'

THOMAS HORSLEY (1462-1545) CORN MERCHANT AND MERCHANT ADVENTURER

Merchant Adventurers, from the 15th century, were overseas traders, particularly in wool and corn. Horsley bequeathed money to found a 'hyghe skull' in a building in St Nicholas' church-yard, later to become the Royal Grammar School and was Mayor of Newcastle in 1514, 1519, 1524, 1525 and 1533. The school moved to the Westgate site in 1607.

SIR PETER RIDDELL (-1641) HOSTMAN, MAYOR AND MP

The riverside area of Tyneside between St Lawrence's and St Anthony's became known as St Peter's, it is thought, following the granting of a lease for a quay (for shipment of coal) to Sir Peter Riddell by Newcastle Corporation in 1630. 'Sir Peter' over the years became 'St' Peter.

SIR JOHN MARLEY (1590-1673) HOSTMAN, MAYOR AND MP

He was the Mayor of Newcastle who withstood a three months siege by the Scottish army in 1644 before being forced to surrender. For its gallant defence Charles I is said to have conferred on the town the motto: 'Fortiter Defendit Triumphans' (triumphing by a brave defence) to accompany its coat of arms. Marley was Mayor of Newcastle five times and is buried in St George's Porch.

RALPH HERON (1765-1786) SON OF A NEWCASTLE ATTORNEY

The unfortunate Ralph Heron was one of those assisting the pioneer aeronaut Lunardi in filling his balloon with gas on the Spital Field, Westgate (now covered by the Central Station). The balloon swayed in the wind and all those holding the guy ropes, except Ralph, were forced to let go. Up he went, entangled in ropes, to a height of at least 500ft before finally falling to his death.

The last interment entered in St Nicholas' Parish Register related to Robert Henderson of Trinity House in 1853. However, six years later the Bewicke vault was opened, by special leave of the Home Secretary, to inter the widow of Calverley Bewicke MP.

St Nicholas' Parish Churchyard

This plan of St Nicholas' Church and surrounding property is the result of a survey in 1770 by Charles Hutton (a local schoolmaster and mathematician). It illustrates the relatively small churchyard before the major town redevelopments of the late 18th century. By 1825 the churchyard covered little more than half an acre and was the smallest in town. The shape of the churchyard suggests it may have begun within the ruins of a temporary Roman camp near the Wall a few centuries before the present church was rebuilt in medieval times.

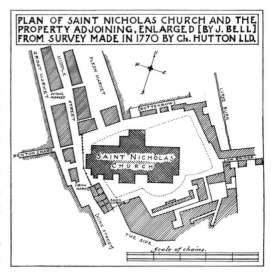

Even in 1300 the churchyard was so overcrowded that the need arose for a building into which human bones could be transferred to allow more outside burials. The resulting 14th century charnel house under part of the north transept is today regarded as one of the best preserved 'bone holes' in England. The charnel house was rediscovered in 1824, the bones reburied elsewhere, and in 1932 converted into a chapel for public use. Burials were revealed below its earthen floor.

The churchyard though open, unenclosed, and not an ideal place around which to live, was conveniently near the town centre. The low overhanging houses had been built so close round the church that only a narrow path existed between them and the churchyard. There are references to 'rubbish and dung piled against the church walls'.

The crypt in 1911, formerly the charnel house.

The churchyard was first enclosed in 1761 when a 'neat and handsome' brick wall with a wooden fence on top was erected by public subscription to tidy up the approach to the church and also provide a more reverent atmosphere for burials. A convenient path for pedestrians encircled the new boundary fence. Over 50 years later iron railings on a stone base (some of which still survive) replaced the earlier boundary. In 1926 a metal frieze, containing biblical phrases in Latin in red gothic script, was added to the railings.

In 1832 several stone coffins and a quantity of

The churchyard in the early 1800s. The levels of the churchyard became higher over the centuries as it was supplemented with soil removed from the inside of the church to create burial vaults.

human bones were discovered under the pavement outside the west door of the church. Following the closure of the churchyard in the mid-1850s more parts of it have disappeared. In 1926 the new parish hall and other buildings were erected on the northern section and a car park now occupies what used to be a popular area for burials, outside the east window. Cathedral Buildings (1901) presently towers over the east end of the church, featuring, above a doorway, a carved rabbit in aggressive mode, presumably added to ward off evil spirits from the churchyard in the same way as gargoyles were meant to centuries earlier.

After many hundreds of interments, including mass burials when plague and cholera were rampant, only a small part of the original churchyard remains. This is in the south west corner. Few headstones remain and several of these have been built into the carpark retaining wall and surrounding paths to the south and east of the church. It is said that the statue of Queen Victoria outside the church covers the burial site of some of the town's cholera victims.

Who's who in St Nicholas' Churchyard

Joseph Barber (1706-1781) Bookseller and copper-plate printer

In his will Joseph Barber directed that his remains be buried in a new vault in the churchyard in 'a strong oak coffin, one inch thick, covered with black baize', that his age and date of death be 'cut deep upon a tombstone', that there should be no pall bearers, and that the coffin should have 'two dovetails across the breast, and be fixed with screw nails' to frustrate potential body snatchers.

Arriving from Ireland in 1740, he opened a shop, among other printers and booksellers, at the north end of the Tyne Bridge and introduced the first copper plate printing 'ever performed in Newcastle'. Six years later he opened the first circulating library in Newcastle at High Bridge and then at larger premises at Amen Corner. Here over 1250 volumes were offered on loan to subscribers, initially at twelve shillings a year and later at 10 shillings following the opening of a rival business. Items sold in the shop included books, prints, tea and 'other commodities'.

Joseph could converse in French, had a knowledge of Latin and Greek, and his clientèle included Thomas Bewick (who printed the above advertisement), John Erasmus Blackett, Charles Brandling, Matthew Ridley and Aubone Surtees. In the 1760s he had a residence built off Westgate Street, amid open fields, which he called Summerhill after his birthplace near Dublin. Although fire destroyed the house in 1773 (suspected arson) the surrounding area became known as Summerhill. He was married three times and fathered six children.

Robert Storey (1733-1822) Surgeon

Robert emigrated to India as a ship's surgeon and became physician to the Nabob of Arcot. He returned home a wealthy man and bought land in east Cramlington in 1791. His daughter and heiress married George Shum who had also made a fortune in India. George Shum-Storey (who took his wife's name) witnessed the Siege of Arcot near Madras and later built Arcot Hall which is now a golf club. Robert's very worn ledger stone lies in the path outside the vestry.

Rev. Robert Wasney (1772-1836) Preacher

'For 25 years the faithful dispenser of the word of God in St Thomas' Chapel in this town, where a monument is erected to his memory by his flock as a testimony of their gratitude for his faithful services.' The chapel of St Thomas stood on Sandhill at the north end of the old Tyne Bridge. It was pulled down in 1830 and worship transferred to the newly built St Thomas' church at Barras Bridge. His headstone is in the path near the seats.

Luigi Grassi (1803-1835) Native of St Giorgio near Como, Italy

Most likely this was the Grassi who, with two others, operated a jewellery and toy warehouse in Dean Street, Newcastle.

Thomas Reevely (1744-1775) Servant

'This stone was erected to his memory by his Master Matthew Bell Jnr. Esq. whom he has served many years faithfully and honestly.'

Matthew Bell was a 'coal-fitter' (another name for a host-man) with an office at the foot of the Ruecastle Chare, Quayside. In 1778, according to the trade directory of that year, there were 20 coal fitters in Newcastle, all with offices on or very near the Quayside. Each fitter was the agent for a specific colliery. Matthew Bell dealt with coals from Willington and Bigge's Main colliery, Wallsend.

GEORGE STEPHENSON (1720-1784)

'Formerly a respectable wharfinger in this town'.

JAMES DAVENPORT (1752-1820) FLAX MERCHANT

He operated a flax mill in the lower Ouseburn Valley on a site until recently occupied by the City Farm, Byker.

JOHN THOMPSON 'CLERK OF THIS CHURCH'

This ledger stone bears sad testimony to the high death rate amongst children. Cholera was endemic as was typhoid and smallpox, and of course all the other childhood diseases that we are protected from today. These are his children.

Elizabeth died an infant
George died an infant
John died March 13th 1791 aged 8
William died April 27th 1791 aged 6
James died May 5th 1791 aged 2

ST NICHOLAS' CEMETERY

BACK WINGROVE AVENUE, FENHAM

At first sight it seems odd that the original and imposing south-west entrance to this five acre cemetery is approached today from the back lane of Wingrove Avenue, Fenham. When opened in 1857 there were no surrounding housing estates or roads, merely open fields with the only access from the Newcastle-Carlisle turnpike, which lay a quarter of a mile to the south, down a minor road.

At that time this minor road lay between the Workhouse 'for the able bodied poor' of 1839 (later Newcastle General Hospital) and Wingrove House, the home, for many years, of John Wigham Richardson the shipbuilder.

Both of the tall vehicle gate pillars are surmounted by large stone seahorses each holding a shield. One depicts a shipwreck and the other a ship in full sail. There is obviously a connection between the seahorses (they denote Newcastle as a seaport in the city coat of arms) and the fact that St Nicholas is the patron saint of seafarers.

A.M. Dunn, architect, planned the cemetery and designed the Dissenters' Chapel to the west and the Established Church Chapel to the east. He also designed, with E.J. Hansom, the tower and steeple for St Mary's RC Cathedral in 1872.

Halfway along the western side of the cemetery was the Smugglers Hole where, in 1822, two illicit stills were discovered down

St Nicholas' Cemetery, Fenham.

a disused coalshaft containing 'about 200 gallons of wash, a long brick chimney, and complete distillery apparatus valued approximately at £50'. Coal and water were readily available nearby. A few days after the discovery, three inquisitive young men were lost for at least 12 hours in the underground passages and only survived thanks to the knowledge of local pitmen answering alarm signals.

Nearly 23,600 people have been buried here. Both chapels are now disused.

WHO'S WHO IN ST NICHOLAS' CEMETERY

REV. CLEMENT MOODY (1811-1871) MA

Clement Moody was the last vicar of Newcastle to occupy the vicarage in Westgate Street. In the early 1860s the picturesque vicarage and its large garden were replaced by the extension of Grainger Street (see photograph on page 35). The vicarage moved to 23 Elswick Villas, Rye Hill. Moody arrived from Carlisle aged 42 and was Vicar of Newcastle

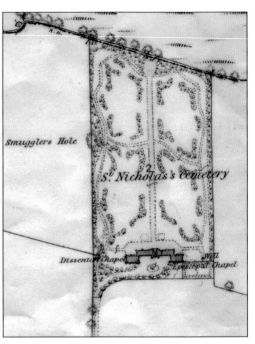

The rural situation of St Nicholas' cemetery, and the Smugglers Hole from the first edition OS map, 1860.

for 18 years. There is a window which cost £500 in St Nicholas' church in his remembrance. He was a very caring man and during the 1853 cholera epidemic he reputedly dealt with 60-80 letters of condolence each day.

DR JOSEPH COLLINGWOOD STEWART (1881-1958) FRCS

During the First World War, Captain Joseph Collingwood Stewart acted as surgeon at Coxlodge Hospital, Gosforth as the wounded returned from the trenches. He became the first consultant surgeon and physician at the newly named Wingrove Hospital (previously the Union Workhouse Hospital) in 1921 and remained in post for 30 years.

St John the Baptist Parish Church

Grainger Street West

The church of St John the Baptist is essentially a 15th century building with more recent restorations. Its origin is most likely 12th century, as evidenced by a narrow round headed window in the north wall of the chancel and other Norman fragments existing in the nave. Building alterations in the 19th century revealed the re-use of early grave covers and a water basin as construction materials. They were probably contemporary with the church's foundation in Norman Times.

St John's, early 19th century.

Who's who in St John's Church

In 1875, during a so-called restoration, many floor gravestones were covered with concrete and tiled. Some were removed to the churchyard and others destroyed. No record of their inscriptions (or situation) was ever prepared. Finally in 1968-72 the church flooring was completely renewed leaving no trace of former memorials. However, other records show that there certainly are many still at rest beneath the floor of the church, including the following:

In 1502 John Vergoose requested that 'his body may be buried in the church of St John in Newcastle before the altar of St Thomas the Martyr' – which cost him 6s 8d towards repairing the fabric of the church.

In 1544 Nicholas Carr asked to be buried in St John's 'as nigh unto the place where his wife was buried as possibly could be'.

In 1571 John Wilkinson (merchant draper, Sheriff 1555, Mayor 1561) wished his body to be buried in St John's Church 'nygh where the organes doithe stande'. This is the first reference to an organ in Newcastle after the Reformation. His will included that 40 shillings be 'delt and gevyn to the poore'.

In 1576 Cuthbert Nicholson, late servant to William Dods of Newcastle, Tanner, directed that his body be buried in St John's church 'as near his mother as might be'.

In 1581 Humphrey Millerson of Benwell, Yeoman, desired to be buried in St John's Church near his father.

In 1623 Oswald Chaitor, linen weaver and parish clerk of St John's for 41 years, was buried in the chancel of the church he had served so long, where there was a gravestone inscribed to his memory.

In 1757 Thomas Matfield (or Matfin), a 14 year old boy, was nearly buried alive in St John's. The funeral cortège from his Low Friar Street home reached St John's church and the funeral hymn was sung in the church porch by his friends from St John's Charity School. Their shrill voices caused the coffin to move and the terrified pall-bearers asked for it to be opened. Thomas, dressed in a shroud, began to stir from a coma. He was taken home, given a glass of cherry brandy and put to bed. Later he became a keelman, finally to die in All Saints poor-house in 1820, aged 77, and be interred in All Saints churchyard (see page 59).

The remains of Adam Askew, an eminent physician, were deposited in his family vault in St John's Church on 19 January 1773. After practising for 50 years in Newcastle he had acquired an immense fortune. The Askew family owned the Redheugh Estate from 1748 to the 1880s and Askew Road, Gateshead, is named after them. A memorial plaque exists in the south transept.

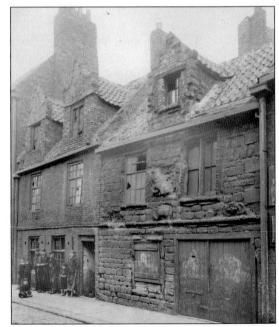

Old houses in Low Friar Street, 1885.

Some Wall Tablets:

Nathaniel Clayton (1709-1786), chancel, north wall

The son of a merchant adventurer he studied theology at Cambridge and acted as lecturer (preacher) at St John's for 50 years along with other religious appointments. He lies buried somewhere within the church. A son and a grandson both qualified as lawyers and together they served a total of 82 years as Newcastle's Town Clerk. Clayton Street is named after the grand-son, John, following his involvement with the Grainger development.

Richard and Rachel Grainger, nave, south wall

Richard Grainger will be remembered as the principal developer of central Newcastle in the 1830s. Although St John's was their parish church, husband and wife were not buried there. Rachel died in Scotland in 1842 immediately after giving birth to her 13th child, who, two days later, followed her to her Lanarkshire grave. She was 42 years old. Ten years later mother and child were re-interred in the family vault at Benwell churchyard. Richard Grainger was buried at St James', Benwell, in 1861 (see page 101).

Thomas Menham (1715-1782), south transept

An ironmonger at the Close. His son later operated the Busy Cottage Iron works in what is now Jesmond Dene.

And memorial windows:

William Hardcastle (1794-1860) Surgeon at Westgate Street, south transept

One of his apprentices, John Snow, became a pioneer anaesthetist and successfully assisted Queen Victoria in the birth of two of her later children. Snow also established the cause of the cholera epidemics – polluted water supplies. Hardcastle and his wife died after the closure of St John's Churchyard and lie interred in Jesmond Old Cemetery.

John Cunningham (1729-1773) The Pastoral Poet, south transept

Interred in the attached churchyard where an inscribed table monument covers his grave, see page 33.

Although no visible reminder remains in the church, the eminent wood engraver Thomas Bewick was married here in 1786 and it is also where some of his children were baptised.

ST JOHN'S PARISH CHURCHYARD

Before 1762 the churchyard had been in an untidy state but in that year it was decided to enclose it with a brick wall with suitable railings above. Around the inside of this wall were planted elm and lime trees. Some gravestones were removed from their original sites. A few gravestones from inside the church were moved to the churchyard. The cost of all this work was met by a subscription from worshippers.

A painting of St John's c.1860 shows the entrance to St John's Lane or Copper Alley 'a narrow dirty place' that existed before Grainger Street was extended towards the Central Station.

In 1784 St John's Lane (now covered by Grainger Street West) was formed to link Bigg Market and Westgate Street (now Westgate Road). The new thoroughfare was made across part of the churchyard, and simultaneously, the north-west corner of the church's north aisle was removed and the aisle shortened. In 1825 the churchyard measured 2,913 square yards (just over half an acre) although originally it probably was nearer the more usual 'God's acre'.

In 1904 there was a serious proposal to remove the church and its burial ground and develop the Grainger Street West site for commercial purposes. A new church was to have been built in the Blenheim Street area out of a compensation package of £300,000. Fortunately the plans collapsed.

During World War II contingency plans were made, in the event of a German invasion, to bury 'a small but vital component of the printing press' belonging to the Newcastle Chronicle and Journal under a table tombstone chosen quickly and at random in the dark in the nearby St John's churchyard. Next day, when the site was re-visited in daylight to confirm its suitability, the person privy to the scheme was astonished to find the chosen tombstone belonged to Thomas Slack who, nearly 180 years earlier, had founded the *Newcastle Chronicle*. Sadly, this tombstone is now one of many missing churchyard memorials.

The construction of a parish hall in 1957 involved the lifting of some gravestones and the opportunity was taken to transform a 'beastly looking' churchyard into a 'green oasis' at an estimated cost of £5,870. In 1990 the churchyard was landscaped. Today very few memorials remain and the ultimate fate of over 300 gravestones is unknown.

WHO'S WHO IN ST JOHN'S CHURCHYARD

RALPH WATERS SENIOR (1720-1798) ARTIST

Born in North Shields, the son of a gardener, Brand's 'History of Newcastle' contains several of Waters' engravings. A colleague of Thomas Bewick, the wood engraver, one of his most popular paintings is 'St Nicholas' Church from the South East'. His table-top grave is at the west end of the churchyard.

St Nicholas' Church from the South East.

JOHN CUNNINGHAM (1729-1773) PASTORAL POET

Born in Dublin, the son of a Scottish wine cooper, his education was interrupted by his father's bankruptcy. With no regular employment and idle habits, he frequented the theatre and had hoped for a stage career but unfortunately lacked talent. He did play some minor parts, often as an eccentric Frenchman, and eked out other earnings by writing in verse for the *Newcastle Chronicle* whose editor and publisher, Thomas Slack, always kept an open door for him. He walked to London to present David Garrick, the renowned actor, with a bound copy of his poems. Garrick was not impressed – he gave Cunningham two guineas and remarked, 'players, sir as well as poets, are always poor'. Shocked at this rejection, Cunningham took to drink, writing a song in praise of beer including the line 'Bid adieu to your folly, get drunk and be jolly'. He died in lodgings in Union Street (between Cloth and Groat Market). Thomas Slack paid for an inscribed ledger stone which survived until 1887 and Joseph Cowen paid for a

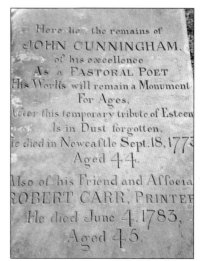

stained glass window in the church's south transept. The present tombstone was unveiled in 1887 by Dr Thomas Hodgkin and financed by public subscription.

St John's Churchyard was noted for its 'poets' corner'. Unfortunately, apart from John Cunningham (above) their memorial stones are now missing. They included Edward Chicken (1698-1747) a schoolmaster, poet, and author of 'The Collier's Wedding'; Thomas Thompson (1773-1816), timber-merchant and songwriter, whose humorous songs in pure dialect included 'Canny Newcassel' and William Watson (1796-1840) whose many songs included 'Dance to thy Daddy'.

ANNE SLACK (1719-1778) : HOSTESS, WRITER, PRINTER, BOOKSELLER

Born in Cumberland, Anne Fisher married Thomas Slack (also a Cumbrian) at Longbenton in 1751. He was a journalist, printer, publisher and manager for Isaac Thompson who published and part owned the *Newcastle Journal*. In 1763 he opened a print shop, the Printing Press, in Middle Street, which also sold books, spectacles, and lottery tickets. In 1764 Thomas established the *Newcastle Chronicle*, a weekly four-page news

Thos Slack

sheet, probably encouraged by Anne as this enabled her own educational text books to be advertised. Their shop became a literary club visited by local writers, actors, artists and politicians. The *Chronicle* remained under family control for the next 86 years until taken over by Joseph Cowen. Anne Slack gave birth to nine daughters, eight of whom survived infancy. Six are buried in St John's churchyard with their parents, though Anne's stone is missing. Another daughter, Sarah, married Solomon Hodgson who carried on the *Newcastle Chronicle* business and is buried nearby.

SOLOMON HODGSON (1761-1800) PRINTER, NEWSPAPER PROPRIETOR

Born in Cumberland, he was probably apprenticed as a letter press printer to Thomas Slack, founder of the *Newcastle Chronicle*. Following Slack's death, he acted as its reporter, editor, advertising agent and publisher at Union Street. He also managed a printing and bookselling business and an agency for patent medicines in the nearby Groat Market.

As a friend of Thomas Bewick, the wood engraver, he helped compile the *General History of Quadrupeds*. Following his early death aged 39 his widow Sarah, Thomas Slack's daughter, also buried here, carried on the business. Their son Thomas continued the *Chronicle* as proprietor and editor for another 43 years after his mother's death in 1822. There is a 96 word epitaph on the table tomb.

GENERAL BURIALS

The parish register of St John's was begun in 1587-8 and the earliest recorded burial occurred on the 3rd January when 'Margrett Stafford, the wiff to Nicholas (Stafford) burried'. By this time unrecorded burials had been taking place for centuries.

In 1589 plague in Newcastle accounted for 1,827 deaths of which 340 were buried in St John's Churchyard. One local historian notes that to escape infection 'hundreds of townspeople retired to towers and platforms of the wall, fields at the Barras Bridge and meadows round St

Westgate Street around 1860. St John's Lane is marked by a break in the wall in the centre of the photograph. The wall to the left is the boundary of the Vicarage (St Nicholas') and its garden – as large a site as St John's and its churchyard. The Vicarage and garden were removed in the 1860s to create the extension to Grainger Street. The remains of the Vicarage pump are at the foot of St John's Lane.

Ann's chapel.' Trade was at a standstill and all the community were affected. Among the victims were the curate of St John's, the grave digger, and the town fool: 'August 1589 Edward Errington the townes fooll buried 23 August in St John's Churchyard, died in the peste'. Fools (eccentric, or odd-looking people) were kept at the expense of the Corporation and other payments relating to them in the town's books included 'cloaths,' 'a long cote' and 'the mendinge of a sore legg'.

In January 1598 Elizabeth Nicolson was buried in St John's Churchyard. She was drowned 'in the Bigg Marcott pant' (the public fountain in the Bigg Market).

Prisoners from the county of Northumberland, executed at the Castle or outside the Westgate, were usually buried in St John's churchyard. The Castle site had, since 1400, been an 'island' governed by Northumberland within the town of Newcastle. Town executions, on the other hand, were normally carried out at Gallowgate and the corpses buried at St Andrew's churchyard. 'Buried in St John's Churchyard, Clement Roderforthe, gentleman, was executed in the castle the 22nd day of August 1599'. In 1613 'another 6 burials following execution in the castle'. On August 11th 1744, three individuals were hanged outside the Westgate, 'two for coining and the other for horse stealing'. They were all buried the same day in St John's churchyard, 'the coiners in one grave'.

Some workmen discovered 'the body of a teenage female without a head, and only a coarse cloth wrapped round it, part of which was much stained with blood' a few inches below the surface of the north side of St John's Churchyard. A reward of twenty guineas was offered by Newcastle Corporation but no conviction ever followed – the body was re-interred in 1786.

The dead bodies of two females were discovered in the coach-office of the Turf Hotel, just down the road from St John's, on Collingwood Street, in November 1828. The packages were addressed to different people in Edinburgh – one had come by the 'Highflyer' coach from York and the other was brought by a local man to be booked through to Edinburgh. It was thought both bodies had been destined for the medical school in that city. Following an inquest by the Newcastle coroner and with neither body showing marks of violence they were both interred in St John's churchyard. No one was charged with the crime.

ST JOHN'S CEMETERY

ELSWICK

St John's cemetery was opened 22nd October 1857 and consecrated on 25th October 1858. The architects were Johnstone & Knowles. The gateway is Gothic style with a Tudor arch supported by tall octagonal piers. A pair of plain lodges flank the entrance, one of which is still in use as an office. In the centre of the cemetery are two gothic chapels, the West Chapel for Church of England and the East Chapel for Dissenters, both dilapidated and out of use.

St John's is the largest cemetery in Newcastle at about 28 acres. Due to the difficult and sloping nature of the terrain, the site was bought for a bargain £800. In 1857 part of the cemetery was enclosed and sold to the Jewish community for £500. This walled enclosure contains the founders of the community in Newcastle and is now full, with over 1,000 graves. In the early 20th century, the size of the cemetery was increased by the addition of a large field to the west of the original site. Nearly 105,000 people have been interred there since it opened.

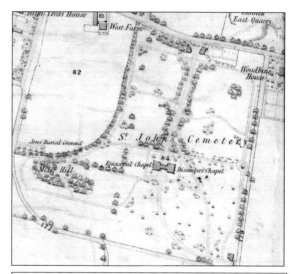

St John's Cemetery from the first edition OS map, 1860, and an early view of the cemetery chapels, below.

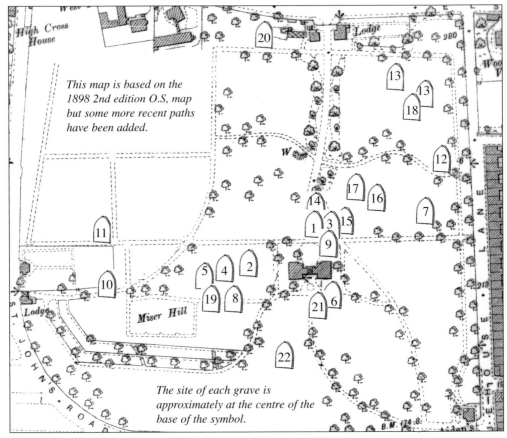

This map is based on the 1898 2nd edition O.S, map but some more recent paths have been added.

The site of each grave is approximately at the centre of the base of the symbol.

1. George Angus	12. Dr John Hunter Rutherford
2. Mary Carmichael	13. John and Robert Sinclair
3. Thomas Cooke	14. Sir William Haswell Stephenson
4. George Cruddas	15. William Stewart
5. Dr Charles John Gibb	16. John Woodger
6. Jushichii Takezo Fukamachi	17. A Chinese headstone
7. Dr Charles Fox Larkin	18. Sir Riley Lord
8. William Mather	19. William Rochester Pape
9. Dr John Theodore Merz	20. Sir Benjamin Chapman Browne
10. Montagu Pit Disaster Memorial	21. John Frederick Weidner
11. Alfonse Reyrolle	22. Fire Brigade Memorial

Who's who in St John's Cemetery

George Angus (1821-1890) India rubber king

Alexander Angus fled Scotland in the 16th century because of religious persecution against Baptists and settled on Tyneside as a leather worker. He was the first of successive generations of skinners and glovers in Newcastle. In 1788 a leather business was founded by Joseph (grandfather of George) and by 1810 his son, William had joined him to process leather from raw hide to the finished article. In 1836 15 year old George was apprenticed to his father, William, as a currier. In 1843 India Rubber was added to leather as a trading material and soon the successful business moved to larger premises on the corner of Grey Street and Market Street. In 1867 a catastrophic fire broke out on Grey Street causing £60,000 damage. A new purpose built factory, 'artistic and commodious', known as St John's Works, was constructed behind  Grainger Street West. The business expanded to Liverpool where the leather warehouse became

Fire rages on Grey Street in August 1867. George Angus's premises were gutted.

the largest in Europe. There were also branches in America. In 1880 Sir Joseph Swan (a friend of the Angus family) staged the first public demonstration of electric lighting in the show window of the Grainger Street West building.

By the 1960s Angus's were the 'largest manufacturer of fire hoses in the world.' Blessed with a family of 13 children, there were always sons and grandsons to carry on the business. George Angus died at Gosforth Low Hall aged 69. In the 1960s the Grainger Street West site closed and the factory moved to Cramlington New Town. George Angus & Co. Ltd merged with Dunlop Ltd as Dunlop Angus Industrial Group in 1968.

MARY CARMICHAEL (1805-1881) WIFE OF J.W. CARMICHAEL
THE PAINTER

Mary Sweet, 'a gentle mannered pretty woman', married artist John Wilson Carmichael (1799-1868) in 1826 at Holy Cross Church, Ryton. As they left the church, news arrived that her husband's studio in the New Road (City Road today) had been burned to the ground. The easygoing Carmichael replied 'well, we can begin all over again', which they did. For the next 20 years they lived at varying addresses on Tyneside. In 1846 they moved to London and Carmichael enjoyed considerable success as the 'celebrated marine painter'. He then obtained three years' work for the *Illustrated London News* and lived in the Baltic Sea area as an unofficial war artist. John and Mary's health suffered in London and they moved to Scarborough in 1864 where John died in 1868 aged 69. Mary returned to Newcastle and in 1869 was living as a haberdasher at Marlborough Crescent. She died in 1881 aged 76. Their youngest daughter Frances Foster (1846-1894) is buried with her mother.

Carmichael's view of North Shields, 1820s.

Thomas Cooke (1835-1914) Businessman

Thomas Cooke began his working life in humble circumstances as an auctioneer's clerk in Market Street. He later moved into banking and property development, eventually becoming a pawnbroker in Pink Lane with a house in nearby Summerhill Street. In 1891 he bought and transformed the corner of Pilgrim Street and Blackett Street into a

palatial building in the classical Renaissance style (by James Cackett) with a graceful oriel window to which a bracket clock and golden lady (nicknamed 'love on tick') were added in 1932. The shop became the Northern Goldsmiths. It claimed to have the first electric lift in Newcastle.

The company supplied chronometers to Shackleton's Polar Expeditions and later to the Admiralty during the first world war.

Eleven years later Cooke opened a similar styled building on the island site at the junction of Westgate Road and Clayton Street West. He also master-minded a tall building on the north side of Blackett Street where his initials 'TC' can still be seen high up on the facade. In another of his developments two new streets near the General Hospital, Crossley Terrace and Sidney Grove, were named after his sons. Thomas Cooke married the sister of James Crossley Eno, the fruit salts inventor, and lived the latter part of his life at Grainger Park Road. For many years he was a magistrate and JP and for a short period served as a town councillor. With others, he was instrumental in acquiring what is now Elswick Park, for the benefit of the public.

Corner of Blackett Street, Newcastle-on-Tyne. 1892

GEORGE CRUDDAS (1788-1879) INDUSTRIALIST AND FINANCIER

George Cruddas started off as a woollen and linen draper in North Shields. In 1845 he formed the Whittle Dene Water Co. with W.G. Armstrong, the great engineer and arms manufacturer, plus three others, and in 1846 the Newcastle Cranage Co. Cruddas later managed the finance department of Sir W.G. Armstrong, Mitchell & Co. Ltd with expertise and was also one of its founders. He died at Elswick Dene aged 91. His son W.D. Cruddas followed in his father's footsteps by controlling financial affairs during the company's period of major expansion and, in 1890, gave land in Scotswood to the town as a recreation ground for the neighbourhood to be called 'the Cruddas Recreation Ground'. It later became known as Cruddas Park.

DR CHARLES JOHN GIBB (1824-1916) SURGEON AND GP

'Sum went to the dispensary, an' sum to Doctor Gibb's,
An' sum to the Informary to mend their broken ribs'

As one of Newcastle's best known GPs, Dr Gibb never retired and continued to work almost up to the day of his death, aged 92. The son of a surgeon, born near Glasshouse Bridge, Ouseburn, he qualified as a surgeon following an apprenticeship at Gateshead Dispensary and the Forth Infirmary.

After travels abroad, his medical career began in earnest when he was appointed, aged 25, as resident house surgeon at the Forth Infirmary.

He began a private practice at 45 Westgate Street in 1854 where he charged a nominal fee of 2s 6d to all patients, rich or poor. Eight years later, during the development of Grainger Street West, he had a modern residence, known today as Gibbs Chambers, built on Westgate Street in the garden of St Nicholas' vicarage (see photograph on page 35). Here he installed a speaking tube from the front door to his bedroom for night emergencies – a forerunner of modern communication systems. Around this time he featured in the *Blaydon Races* song and there is a suggestion this was a planned self advertisement. His popularity soared, with many travelling long distances to con-

sult him. He was also summoned to the houses of the wealthy by special message. In an urgent case, it was not unusual for him to charter a special train.

Dr Gibb moved to Villa Real, Sandyford (later renamed Sandyford Park, and later still Nazareth House) aged almost 60, and died there 33 years later. During this time he continued to practise as a GP at Gibbs Chambers and would often be seen stepping into his carriage, carrying his leather bag containing the day's takings, on his way back to Sandyford Park. Dr Gibb was a widower and left two married daughters.

JUSHICHII TAKEZO FUKAMACHI (1856-1886) PAYMASTER IN THE IMPERIAL JAPANESE NAVY

Paymaster of the Japanese cruiser *Naniwa*, he died of injuries as a result of a fall on board while at Jarrow Slake (in preparation for leaving the Tyne). The *Naniwa* had been launched at Mitchell's Low Walker Yard in 1885.

DR CHARLES FOX LARKIN (1800-1879) SURGEON, ORATOR & POLITICAL REFORMER

Considered by many as the greatest orator to have lived in the north of England, Charles Fox Larkin was also one of its most fiery and effective political agitators.

A native of London, he was born in the same house (and room) as Charles James Fox the 18th century politician. The son of an Irish Catholic father, at one time a gardener at Ravensworth Castle and then landlord of the Black Boy pub in the Groat Market, young Charles was destined by his parents for the priesthood. While at Ushaw College he decided on a career change and became apprenticed to a Newcastle surgeon, William Ingham. He practised at various Newcastle addresses for the rest of his life, and, but for his outspoken and radical views, would probably have reached high office in the medical profession.

In 1831 he was one of a few speakers to address a crowd of 50,000 on Newcastle Town Moor concerning parliamentary reform, and later urged the non-payment

of taxes until the Bill became law. When it was proposed to close the Central Exchange News Room on Sundays in 1842 (because of violation of the fourth commandment) Larkin protested that the Old Testament should be irrelevant to non-Jews and considered entirely out of date. On another occasion, two years later, he campaigned against the proposal that admission to the opening of St Mary's Catholic Cathedral would be by ticket only.

His memorial today is a sad reflection of what it was like when unveiled by Joseph Cowen MP before an estimated 1,000 onlookers. The classically designed monument by Thomas Oliver junior once contained a bust of Larkin under its canopy with an urn above (illustrated). The epitaph, now badly eroded reads: 'The orator is gone, and from this hour hath passed a voice, a presence, and a power.'

WILLIAM MATHER (1787-1863) BUILDER AND MILLIONAIRE

By far the most spectacular monument in the cemetery belongs to the Mather family whose fairy tale rise to fabulous wealth occurred towards the end of 1836. The origin of their wealth can be traced back to an Alexander Adams who, as a Newcastle hostman for the Montagu Main and Whitefield Colliery, bequeathed 'an immense fortune' to an only son living in Calcutta, India, in 1816. This son died unmarried and the wealth then passed on to Thomas Naters,

a cousin on his mother's side, resident of New York USA, and then Switzerland. Thomas Naters died in November 1836 and bequeathed the remainder of his inheritance to William Mather – nearly £300,000 – making him a millionaire in today's money. The *Newcastle Journal* described these windfalls as 'freaks of fortune'.

Up to this time William Mather, a builder and bricklayer, had been living in typical artisan housing at addresses such as Forth Street and Stowell Street. After his windfall he moved to 5 Eldon Square and is described as a 'gentleman' – presumably retired at the early age of 49. Twenty years later he was living in style at Beech Grove, Elswick, a large Jacobean style house demolished in the 1890s. A street nearby has been named Mather Street.

At Christmas 1836 William Mather's name appears in the press as donating £5 for the benefit of debtors in Newcastle gaol and a few years later he is recorded attending the Hanover

Square Chapel: 'William Mather afterwards millionaire'.

It is not known precisely what the relationship was between Mather, Adams and Naters but William Mather's two eldest sons bore their names. William Adams Mather was born in 1831 and the second son was baptised Charles Thomas Naters Mather in 1832.

The high plinth of the vaulted tomb supports an arcaded canopy with much Gothic tracery and decoration and is listed as a Grade II structure. The vault contains the remains of William and his three sons. The mausoleum covers a relatively large site (18 grave spaces) and was once much more imposing. There had been a lead-covered dome, patterned tiles surrounding the base and bronze chains and posts enclosing the structure. Additionally there were figures and a cross decorating the area under the canopy.

Dr John Theodore Merz (1840-1922) Industrialist, scientist and scholar

Born in Manchester, the son of a headmaster, he went to university in Germany. A pioneer of the electrical supplies industry he also had an interest in chemicals and other industries. As a founder of the Newcastle Upon Tyne Electric Supply Company, a director of the Swan Electric Light Company, Chairman of the Tyneside Tramways and Tramroads Company, to name but a few, his interest lay in the industrial application of electricity for lighting, power and transport.

Merz married Alice Mary Richardson and immediately gained three high profile Quaker brothers in law: John Wigham Richardson (shipbuilder), Robert Spence Watson (solicitor and prominent local liberal) and Thomas Pumphrey (grocer and coffee dealer).

With others Merz provided cash to help found 'The College of Physical Science' at Newcastle in 1871. He later became its principal. To enable the first stage of the Armstrong Building to go ahead he pledged personal securities and today his name is remembered at Newcastle University in 'Merz Court', a building containing the faculty of Electrical, Electronic and Chemical Engineering.

A mathematician of the highest order, Merz was also a writer. An active member of the 'Lit & Phil' for over 50 years he gave many lectures and became vice president in 1913.

His son Charles Hesterman Merz, an electrical engineering consultant, often described as 'the British Edison', carried on his father's work and forged the much respected partnership of Merz and McLennan, known worldwide for its excellence. During World War I Charles Merz was engaged on anti-submarine work for the Admiralty, refusing honours and payment because of his Quaker beliefs. Tragedy struck in World War II when his London home received a direct hit killing him, his two children, and some of his household staff.

THE MONUMENT TO THE MONTAGU VIEW PIT DISASTER 1925

On 30th March 1925 148 men and boys went to work as usual at the Montagu View Pit, Scotswood, little realising they were in imminent danger and that some of them only had hours left to live. They never knew that only a thin wall of coal, six inches thick was holding back three and a half million gallons of foul, putrid pit water lying in the adjacent Paradise pit, last used in 1848. The recommended thickness for dividing walls was 40 yards but due to haphazard plans of underground workings and over 70 years of inactivity, the Montagu management were unaware of the potential danger.

The first sign of trouble was the blackout of safety lamps due to clouds of 'black damp' which suffocated several miners and plunged the working area into darkness. Then suddenly an inrush of water submerged all escape routes and many miners were drowned.

It was seven weeks before the first of the bodies was recovered and a further five months before the last of the 38 victims was removed. Thirteen pit ponies also lost their lives. Identification of corpses proved difficult, but clues such as individual trouser patches, home knitted stocking tops, leather belts and teeth eventually solved the problem. Rescuers with breathing apparatus were required to swim though polluted water to reclaim bodies, coffin them on the spot and then float them back on rafts. The main funeral took place in heavy rain on 24th May when 50,000 lined the 2.5 mile route to the cemetery. Other funerals took place later.

Waiting for news at Montagu Pit.

The Montagu View Pit never re-opened and later a cattle market occupied the site. New mining legislation eventually came into force. Owners of adjoining collieries were required to exchange plans and all information relating to abandoned workings was to be deposited at a newly created Mines Department.

Various relief funds were set up. One of these schemes involved the raffle of a new free-hold house on Newcastle's West Road organised by the owners of the *Newcastle Daily Chronicle*. Tickets cost a shilling each and the competition was to guess how many passengers travelled on Newcastle trams on 30th May 1925. The house became known as the 'shilling' house and was built of reinforced concrete in the form of a roman milecastle or turret with a flat roof. It was initially valued at £1500.

The tall freestone cross, unveiled in June 1926 by the president of the Northumberland Miners Association, shows the Good Shepherd on one side of the column and a miner in working clothes on the other.

Crowds line Elswick Road as the main funeral arrives at St John's Cemetery, May 1925.

ALPHONSE CONSTANT REYROLLE (1864-1919) MANUFACTURER OF ELECTRICAL ENGINEERING EQUIPMENT

The son of a French soldier, Alphonse Reyrolle emigrated to London aged 19 to work in a firm of scientific instrument makers. Soon he was making his own goods for electrical firms in his own factory and quickly gained a reputation for excellent workmanship.

Reyrolle came to Tyneside in 1901, probably because of the early development of the electricity supply industry. J.T. Merz, the electrical pioneer, and Sir Charles Parsons, developer of the steam turbine, were already well established. He founded A. Reyrolle & Co Ltd at Hebburn with 58 employees. By his death some 18 years later, the payroll had grown to 700. Reyrolle enjoyed an early monopoly of the production of switchgear, considered safe from the risk of fire and explosions, for use in coal mines, power stations and warships. It was not long before Reyrolle's became a worldwide household name.

It is said Reyrolle personally inspected every new pattern produced in the works and, although essentially an organiser and developer rather than a dedicated inventor, he was not above rolling up his sleeves and showing that he was essentially a practical man with especial care for the apprentices, 'my boys'. Married with one son he lived for several years at Netherton Lodge, Beech Grove Road, beside Elswick Park.

DR JOHN HUNTER RUTHERFORD (1826-1890) EVANGELIST, PHYSICIAN AND EDUCATIONALIST

Born in Jedburgh, the son of a labourer, John Hunter Rutherford trained for the Presbyterian ministry but turned to evangelism. As a visiting preacher he travelled widely in Scotland and England before settling, aged 24, in Newcastle, where poverty and drunkenness were already major problems. His preaching

on the Quayside, Town Moor and then in the lecture room of the Music Hall Building in Nelson Street was so popular that a subscription list was opened in 1860 to build a new church, to seat 1200, in Bath Lane.

Wishing to improve health care in the Newcastle slums, he became (aged 41) both a physician and surgeon. During the Franco-Prussian War of 1870 he assisted the Red Cross on the continental battlefields. Alongside his preaching, he operated a considerable medical practice at Elswick Lodge, Elswick Lane, where the poor received free treatment. Ironically the Rutherford Memorial Fountain, originally unveiled at St Nicholas' Square in 1894 advocating that 'Water is Best' is now situated in the Bigg Market surrounded by the establishments he had objected to so strongly.

The Rutherford Memorial fountain in its original site on St Nicholas' Square, 1900.

Above all Rutherford is probably best remembered for his interest in education. Following the Education Act of 1870 he founded an elementary school in Corporation Street with a large hall and two classrooms for 660 scholars. Several years later a School of Science and Art opened nearby where day pupils paid £4 4s per year. To help fund scholarships the selfless teachers repaid their invigilating fees as contributions. In 1894 Rutherford Memorial College for about 650 boys and girls opened in Bath Lane. Much of its furniture was made on site, there was a café in the basement, and a devoted caretaker dried the clothing of staff and pupils caught in the rain. A new Technical Wing opened alongside this College in 1910 (the foundation stone laid by the polar explorer Sir Ernest Shackleton) to accommodate evening class students. The Grammar School, as it had become, moved to its West Road site in 1956 and ten years later the Technical College transferred to Ellison Place, eventually becoming Northumbria University.

Rutherford promoted relief for the unemployed and his free winter Sunday morning breakfasts continued well into the 20th century. Some say his sudden death at 64 was brought on by financial worries following the failure of the Ouseburn Engine Works which he tried to operate as a workers' co-operative. At his death all Newcastle schools, colleges and libraries closed for the day, Elswick works stopped production at noon, and thousands lined the route to the cemetery from his home at Eldon Square.

Children at Bath Lane School, 1882.

Sadly all associated buildings in Bath Lane and Corporation Street were demolished, but in the foyer of the Ellison Building (University of Northumbria) is preserved a stained glass memorial window taken from the Bath Lane Congregational Church, featuring Rutherford as the Good Samaritan. The adjoining assembly hall of the University became the Rutherford Hall.

JOHN SINCLAIR (1825-1895) ROBERT SINCLAIR (1835-1890)
TOBACCO MANUFACTURERS

Born in Scotland, the Sinclair brothers, John and Robert, settled in Newcastle as young men to trade in partnership, as retail tobacconists, initially in Dean Street and then Nun Street. Later they moved production to a cottage in Temple Court off Blenheim Street.

Their 30 year old partnership ended in 1885 when both partners opened new and separate purpose-built tobacco factories. Robert's building fronted Westgate Road on the Temple Court site and John opened his business in Bath Lane. Today the Westgate Road site, Blenheim House,

Robert Sinclair's memorial.

contains apartments while the Bath Lane building now forms part of the Tyne Brewery.

At the centenary celebrations in 1956, it was estimated they had produced enough of their famous 'Golden Brown Twist' tobacco 'to circuit the world ten times'. Their 'Ladies Twist', a chewing tobacco, proved popular with those not allowed to smoke on duty, such as pitmen and policemen. Tobacco was believed to be a cure for all manner of illnesses and during the Great Plague of 1665 smoking was compulsory at Eton College with masters holding smoking classes for their pupils.

SIR WILLIAM HASWELL STEPHENSON (1836-1918) INDUSTRIALIST

Born at Throckley House to a Wesleyan Methodist family, Stephenson was one of eight children. His father established the

Throckley Fire Clay & Gas Retort Works. Stephenson founded the Throckley Coal Co. (with his brother and John Spencer, iron founder) and went on to become a director of Newcastle and Gateshead Gas Co., Newcastle and Gateshead Water Co., Tyne Steam Shipping Co., Northern Accident Co., Newcastle Grain Warehouse Co., and Scotswood, Newburn & Wylam Railways.

In 1862 he married Eliza Mary Bond and they lived at Summerhill Grove, then Elswick House.

Stephenson was Mayor in 1875, 1884, 1894, 1909, 1910 and 1911 and was Sheriff in 1886. In 1900 he was knighted for services to Newcastle.

A generous benefactor to Newcastle and Methodism, he gave Elswick Library to the city in 1893, Heaton Library in 1898, and Walker Library in 1908.

A preacher throughout adult life, he directed that his home should later be used by the National Children's Home and Orphanage (Elswick House).

Heaton Library, 1898.

WILLIAM STEWART (1826-1886) TEA MERCHANT

William was born in Belford, the son of a builder. He was educated at Mr Thompson's academy in Northumberland Street, and then apprenticed to a grocer. In 1851 he opened a tea dealership on Grainger Street and advertised extensively. Large wooden Chinese figures, made by local wood carving firm T.H Tweedy, with whom the artist Ralph Hedley served his apprenticeship, decorated the shop front. In 1876 Stewart became Sheriff. He died at Fernwood, Clayton Road, Jesmond (later occupied by Sir Walter Runciman). The business was eventually sold to Rington's Tea Company.

ALDERMAN WILLIAM STEWART.

Ward's trade directory for 1867-8 promotes the tea empire.

JOHN WOODGER (1813-1876) INVENTOR OF THE KIPPER

Born in Hampshire, the son of an agricultural labourer, John Woodger moved to Newcastle, aged 27 as a servant, and then went on to run a public house. With great foresight and ingenuity he adapted the 'kippered salmon' (*cypera* is Old English for a spawning salmon) technique to the herring in 1843 after the wooden shed in which he had left some salted herring caught fire. He discovered that the rescued fish were extremely tasty! In 1845, while still a publican, he established a small business with his two brothers. They opened a curing yard at North Shields and a shop in Northumberland Street. In 1851 John split from his brothers and opened up a curing yard at Newbiggin-by-the-Sea with other premises at the foot of Westgate Street, Newcastle. The

business expanded north to Seahouses and down the coast to Great Yarmouth in 1858 to take advantage of an even longer herring season. John owned several properties along the East Coast as well as in Newcastle and spent much time travelling between curing yards, arranging gangs of Scottish girls to gut the herrings.

He gave benevolently to the poor in Great Yarmouth where he owned property, was a Liberal Councillor and also a Guardian but died in Newcastle. Two generations later the much expanded business was acquired by Macfisheries. A holly tree now hides his monument.

A CHINESE HEADSTONE

This Chinese headstone is to the memory of a Chinese sailor who died of tuberculosis on board the transport ship *Hai Shin* at the Elswick Shipyard in 1881. Nearby is a group of three head-stones (now lying face down) relating to the deaths of three Chinese sailors at

Chinese sailors at an Elswick launch.

Newcastle Infirmary six years later. These four headstones were erected in 1887 by the officers and crew of two Chinese cruisers launched at the Elswick Shipyard. Both these vessels, belonging to the Imperial Chinese Navy, were sunk several years later during the war with Japan, whose fleet also included ships built at Elswick.

Chinese funeral custom required the accompanying crew to kneel by each grave where they silently bowed their heads five or six times. Once the grave had been infilled, a heap of joss paper was lit over the mound.

Sir Riley Lord (1837-1920) Rags to riches fundraiser for the new RVI

Born in Accrington, Lancashire, Riley was the son of a block printer. Little lay between the family and poverty and on the death of his father, Riley, aged seven, was put to work in a Lancashire mill (the Act of 1844 banned work for the under-eights but this only stopped Riley's work briefly). Despite this inauspicious start, he attended night classes at the local Mechanics Institute, and, as an ambitious young man, arrived in Newcastle in 1862 as a superintendent of the Prudential Assurance Company. Elected councillor for Byker in 1885, he was instrumental in raising £100,000 (about one third of estimated costs) for the new Royal Victoria Infirmary and was given the honour of laying the foundation stone. He received a knighthood in 1900, and was Mayor of Newcastle twice.

William Rochester Pape (1831-1923) Gunsmith and organiser of the world's first dog show

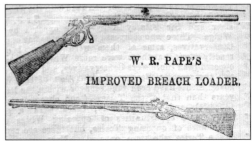

Pape was born in Amble. His father owned a game dealing and fishing tackle shop in Collingwood Street. In 1855 Pape opened his own gunsmith's shop, also in

Collingwood Street, and made many improvements to gun design. In 1859 he organised Britain's first dog show, in Newcastle Corn Exchange in the Groat Market, probably as a way of promoting his gunsmith business. It was a two-day all male show with no women

> **The following are their decisions :—**
> **DOGS.**
> Pointers. Best, one of Pape's celebrated double-barrelled guns, worth from £15 to £20. 1st, J. Brailsford, Esq., Knowsley, Lancashire. Very highly commended—George Atkinson, Esq., Hall Farm, Seaham ; and John Angus, Esq., Percy-street, Newcastle. Highly commended—John Charlton, Newcastle ; Charles Lloyd, Esq., Howick, Alnwick ; and Edward Cowen, Esq., Blaydon. Commended—Charles Hibbert, Esq., Greenbank, Smallshaw, Ashton-under-Lyne ; and Thomas Scott, Longhurst. 23 competitors.
> Setters. Best, one of Pape's celebrated double-barrelled guns, worth from £15 to £20. 1st, William Jobling, Esq., Morpeth, (black and tan). Very highly commended—Thos. Robson, Esq., Ord-street, Newcastle. Highly commended—Thompson Coe, Esq., Middlesborough. Commended—R.

exhibitors and no bitch exhibits allowed. Prizes, sponsored by the *Newcastle Weekly Chronicle*, were only awarded to winners of the 'setter' and 'pointer' classes who each received a Pape double-barrelled gun. An enthusiastic breeder of pointers, Pape's other interests included fishing, falconry and natural history. In 1923, Pape was knocked down by a motor van near his shop. He received head injuries and died three weeks later aged 91.

SIR BENJAMIN CHAPMAN BROWNE (1839-1917)
MARINE-ENGINEER & SHIP BUILDER

Browne, who was was born in Gloucestershire, was the son of a colonel in the 9th Lancers. He began his career as an apprentice mechanical engineer at Elswick Works. Eventually, assisted by his friend, banker Thomas Hodgkin, he purchased the Forth Banks Engine Works of R. & W. Hawthorn. In 1871 he acquired a riverside site and built St Peter's Engine Works. 1885 saw the formation of R. & W. Hawthorn, Leslie & Co Ltd and Browne led the new company as chairman until 1915. He was largely responsible for the company's success in producing marine engines, steam turbines and destroyers for the Admiralty. He also established a valuable trade with Russia in naval vessels. Browne worked with Charles Parsons in the generation of electricity by steam turbine.

Elswick works, mid-19th century.

He was a member of the Institution of Civil Engineers, the Institution of Mechanical Engineers and the Institution of Naval Architects. Browne also helped to establish the first chair of Mechanical Engineering and Naval Architecture at Newcastle's Durham College of Science. As well as being Mayor twice (1885 and 1886), a Justice of the Peace and Deputy Lieutenant of Northumberland, he also received a knighthood in 1887.

JOHN FREDERICK WEIDNER (1853-1934) EXPORT MERCHANT

The son of a Liverpudlian, Weidner was born in Newcastle. He was director of several shipping and industrial enterprises as well as being chairman of Finlay & Co Ltd, tobacconists. He became sheriff in1897 and Lord Mayor in 1912, only the second Roman Catholic to have held the Mayoralty since the Reformation. He was also consul for Venezuela, Panama and Cuba. As a memorial to his son Charles, killed at Ypres in 1917, he gave his home, Heddon House, to the charity of St Vincent de Paul to be used as a Home of Rest. Weidner Road, Fenham, is named after him.

A MEMORIAL TO THREE FIREMEN, 1890

'In commemoration of the tragic deaths of William Murphy, William Bowey and James Grey, members of the Newcastle upon Tyne Fire Brigade, whose lives were sacrificed on the occasion of a fire on the premises of Mawson Swan, chemists, in Mosley Street on September 23rd 1890. The monument was erected 'by their fellow citizens in recognition of heroic duty and admiration of self sacrifice.'

The three firemen died from the effects of inhaling nitric acid fumes.

Fireman James Grey.

ALL SAINTS PARISH CHURCH

PILGRIM STREET

All Saints Church, elliptical in shape, was built in the late 18th century on the west end of the site of the medieval All Hallows (or All Saints) Church. Part of the present burial ground lay under the east end of the medieval church. All Saints parish became the most populous district of Newcastle with both old and new churches each accommodating up to 2,000 worshippers.

The medieval All Hallows Church.

Roger Thornton, well known for his benevolence to the town, worshipped at All Hallows, lived in Broad Chare and was buried inside the church in 1429 under an altar tomb alongside his wife who predeceased him by 18 years. Reputedly he had arrived penniless at Newcastle's West gate in the late 1300s eventually becoming a wealthy Quayside merchant and shipowner. He served the town well on several occasions as Mayor and MP. A memorial brass, of Flemish origin and said to be one of the largest in Britain, later covered the tomb. It showed engraved figures of the couple with their seven sons and seven daughters plus Apostles, saints and symbols. Unfortunately the altar tomb monument disappeared at the time of the church's demolition (1786) but the brass survived and can be seen today inside St Nicholas' cathedral.

When making wills in medieval times it was common to make specific requests for burial within the church:

In 1570 Allan Dixon, a ropemaker, 'directed that his body be buried in the south east nook of the chancel of All Hallows, Newcastle, within the church'.

In 1570 John Havelock 'desired to be buried near his mother-in-law in All Saints church'.

All Saints Churchyard today.

In 1572 George Dent, a gentleman, 'directed that his body be buried within the church of All Saints, Newcastle, before the pulpit, amongst his friends'.

The 'passing bell' which tolled as a person lay dying with a stroke for every year of their age was abolished at All Hallows in 1643 as superstitious, but was reinstated twelve years later due to loss of revenue.

John Wesley is said to have worshipped at All Hallows when in Newcastle in the mid-18th century, finding more communicants there than anywhere else in England except London and Bristol.

In 1785 the south wall of All Hallows nave collapsed and David Stephenson, Newcastle's leading architect at that time, considered it more economical to build a new church than to patch up a structure at least 500 years old. It was stipulated that no graves or vaults were to be made within the new church, as it seemed likely that these had contributed to the instability of the building.

This fine new Georgian church was completed in 1796. To celebrate, a soldier in the Cheshire Militia, John Burdikin, performed a handstand at the top of the steeple, 195 feet above ground level, on a stone 2ft 6ins in diameter, and remained upside down 'for some time'. In 1816, when repairs to the steeple were required, his son, a bricklayer, repeated the same daring feat.

Inside the church is a plaque to the memory of its architect David Stephenson, who died in 1819 aged 63. He was also responsible for the design of Mosley Street, Dean Street and Newcastle's first Theatre Royal in Drury Lane. His table tomb memorial disappeared from the churchyard many years ago.

There is also a mural tablet to the memory of Edward Moises, the only son of Edward Moises, headmaster of Newcastle Grammar School (see page 62). He drowned aged 16 in 1813 in a skating accident on the Town Moor. His watch, which stopped at the time of his drowning, was originally fixed to the mural tablet but is now missing.

The church was deconsecrated in 1961. It reopened in 1996 as Saint Willibrord with All Saints Anglican Catholic Church.

All Saints from the east c.1820.

ALL SAINTS CHURCHYARD

In 1632 Dorothy Lawson, a well known and devoted Catholic was interred in All Hallows churchyard. There was obviously local tolerance of Roman Catholicism because this would never have been permitted in a Puritan stronghold. Under cover of darkness, the 52-year-old was carried in her own boat from her home at St Anthony's, followed by other boats and barges to Newcastle quayside where they were met by civic dignitaries. From there the coffin, covered with a black velvet pall displaying a white satin cross, was carried to the church door, delivered to the Catholics, and then laid with Catholic ceremonies in the unmarked grave at night.

In 1746, as the Jacobite army were expected to arrive in the town, the gravedigger at All Hallows was paid five shillings for 'concealing and securing the church plate' at night, watched by churchwardens with lanterns.

When the 18th century church was built, several adjoining houses were compulsorily purchased and demolished so the churchyard could be extended and enclosed for the first time.

On 8 January 1802, at about one o' clock in the morning, 30 yards of the churchyard's high wall collapsed into Silver Street with a 'tremendous crash'. Many coffins were exposed, together with 'vast quantities of human bones.' An adjoining house was badly damaged, the repairs of which, together with the erection of a new wall, amounted to £249.

Thomas Matfield or Matfin who recovered from a premature funeral in St John's Church (see page 30) is buried in the churchyard in an unmarked grave.

In 1866 the *Northern Daily Express* reported: 'It appears that boys from Silver Street and other low localities adjacent are in the habit of clambering into the churchyard and, not content with using it as a playground, dig up the bones with which the soil teems and dispose of them to the marine store dealers'. The paper stated that a number of skulls and other human remains could be seen lying about the churchyard.

In 1882 much of the churchyard was laid out as a garden for public use.

From the Weekly Chronicle, 1 February 1896.

WHO'S WHO IN ALL SAINTS CHURCHYARD

WILLIAM BATSON (1743-1826) CORN MERCHANT AND BANKER

William Batson, a prominent Newcastle Methodist and businessman, must take some credit for the transformation of Richard Grainger from a jobbing builder into the developer and visionary of later years. As a young man, Grainger's work ethic and personality had impressed Batson to such an extent that in 1819 he offered the 22 year old a contract to build a row of three storey brick houses down one side of a new street, leading off New Bridge Street. Grainger was so eager to make a success of this, his first important commission, that he worked up to 18 hours a day, often beginning as early as 3.00am. This new street, Higham Place, took its name from Batson's country home, Higham Dykes, near Ponteland. Today, unfortunately, only three of the original Georgian houses remain.

Higham Place, marked, stretches north from New Bridge Street in this view of c.1860.

RICHARD BURDON (1721-1810) PUBLICAN, BREWER AND LANDOWNER

One of 12 children, Burdon was baptised at Witton Gilbert. He came to Newcastle to become a publican at the Highlander in Spicer Lane (off Broad Chare) and a leading partner in Burdon's Brewery, also on the Quayside. He owned landed property at Brunton (Gosforth) and lived at 'up market' Shieldfield Green in a substantial house with a spacious garden. He was often to be seen out riding until the last year or two of his long life.

Burdon Terrace, Sanderson Road and Haldane Terrace in Jesmond all derive their names from Richard Burdon and his descendants.

His son Thomas (later Sir) (1758-1826) married Jane Scott, the sister of Lord Eldon and Lord Stowell. Grandson, Richard (1791-1865) married Elizabeth Sanderson, only daughter and heiress of Sir James Sanderson, a former MP and Lord Mayor of London – by Royal License he took the name and arms of Sanderson to become Richard Burdon-Sanderson. Great grandson Richard (1821-1876) married Isabella Mitchelson Haldane of Edinburgh.

JOSEPH GARNETT (1772-1861) CHEMIST, DRUGGIST AND PHILANTHROPIST

Garnett's wish to be buried in this churchyard required Parliamentary approval because of its official closure a few years earlier. Interment in his parents' grave was granted because of the very many local philanthropic activities he was involved with. Remaining a bachelor with a thriving business and a simple lifestyle, he became quite wealthy. It is said he received (and replied to) as many as 40 begging letters daily, made frequent donations to local churches, and bequeathed over £6,000 to local charities.

Born at Alnwick in humble circumstances, he was extremely good at mathematics (winning several competitions), had an excellent command of Latin and Hebrew and was an able musician. His first job was at the Royal Observatory, Greenwich where he invented 'a new semaphore for signalling astronomical messages.'

Eye problems forced him to leave Greenwich and return to Newcastle where he eventually set up business as a chemist and druggist on the Quayside before moving to premises at the foot of Side. Here he remained, living above the shop, until his death 61 years later. This site today is covered by the Akenside Traders pub. Though never a doctor, he advised customers about their complaints and ailments and proved extremely popular.

His memory is perpetuated by a stained glass window in St Nicholas' Cathedral.

DR JOHN HALL MD (1733-1793) PHYSICIAN

The son of a barber surgeon, John Hall practised medicine in Pilgrim Street and, aged 38, became physician to the Infirmary. He took particular interest in mental illness and, in 1766, converted a former residence in Spital Tongues into a private asylum for 'respectable' lunatics. He named it St Luke, probably after the biblical physician. Later it became known as the Bellegrove Retreat and more recently as 'White Knights', a private residence.

Meanwhile the purpose-built municipal Lunatic Asylum (which opened 1767 off Corporation Street) was considered a disgrace, frequently overcrowded, and with cells 'less comfortable than cow houses'. Following Dr Hall's appointment as physician, the building was enlarged and conditions for inmates considerably improved.

Dr Hall teamed up with two surgeons to build public baths, which opened 1781, adjacent to what is now Bath Lane. A contemporary source suggested the baths revived 'the comfort and elegance of the Roman Age in the use of vapour, hot and tepid baths, the swimming basin and the cold enclosed baths'. During the early 19th century, mine workings caused the water supply to disappear and sometime later the site was redeveloped.

A celebrity patient of Dr Hall was John Boswell, a younger brother of Dr Johnson's biographer who, as an army lieutenant, occasionally suffered from insanity.

REV. EDWARD MOISES (1763-1845) HEADMASTER

Rev. Moises was headmaster of Newcastle's Royal Grammar School for 41 years. He specialised in classical literature and Oriental languages. He was only 24 and had no educational experience when he took over the headmastership from his uncle, the Rev. Hugh Moises, who had been in the post for 38 years (see page 19). He retired from his school house at Westgate to live in what is now Jesmond Dene, at a villa named St Mary's Mount (now demolished).

WILLIAM SCOTT (1696-1776) HOSTMAN, PUBLICAN

The son of a shipping clerk, William was apprenticed to a hostman and later prospered in the coal shipping business. He also owned keels and a pub where the keelmen drank. When he died his estate, which included his home in Love Lane and property at Usworth, County Durham, was estimated at £24,000 – a substantial sum.

His first wife, Isabella, died young, having given birth to three children in less than four years of marriage. Ten years later William married Jane Atkinson who was to produce ten more children including three sets of twins. She out-lived William by 24 years. Two of Jane's children were William, later Lord Stowell, and John, later the first Earl of Eldon, who married Bessie Surtees. William's birth, in 1745, was something of an adventure for Jane. Newcastle was anticipating the imminent arrival of the Jacobite army, so the family felt that Jane would be safer at her father's country estate at Usworth, County Durham. By

William Scott's house, Love Lane.

the time the decision was made, Newcastle's town gates were closed and fortified, so there was no option but to lower the heavily pregnant Jane in a basket from the town walls and then row her down river. At Usworth, Jane finally gave birth to William and his twin sister Barbara.

JOHN STOKOE (1756-1836) HOUSE CARPENTER AND ARCHITECT

For much of his working life John was involved in routine build-ing. On the ledgerstone at his wife's death he is described as a 'house carpenter', but when John died, 43 years later, another inscription was added to the stone, referring to him as an 'architect' – professional architects were largely unknown before the early 19th century. John worked on several important projects. Elswick Hall, now demolished, was rebuilt in the classical style in 1803 to the design of John and his father William. John and son William later designed the classical south front of Newcastle Guildhall, which was added in 1809. In 1812, John designed the Moot Hall (illustrated) in the Doric style, and at about the same time he designed a new bridge over the Pandon Burn (now beneath New Bridge Street).

EDWARD WALKER (1768-1831) EDITOR AND PROPRIETOR OF THE NEWCASTLE COURANT

The *Newcastle Courant*, the town's oldest newspaper, and the first newspaper published north of the Trent, began in 1711. It appeared on a weekly basis for almost 200 years before it was absorbed into the *Newcastle Journal*. Initially small in size, measuring only 6ins x 7.5ins, it contained little or no local news, no illustrations, and only the occasional advertisement. For much of this period newspapers were relatively expensive due to a government tax. In 1833 the paper cost 7d (including stamp duty of 4d) and later, even after the price had dropped to threepence halfpenny, some shopkeepers hired out the paper to readers at a halfpenny per hour.

Edward Walker took over the newspaper's publication in 1796 and operated at 54 Pilgrim Street for 35 years until his death aged 63. He is described in trade directories as a 'printer, stationer, patent medicine vendor and publisher of the Hue and Cry' (another name for the *Courant,* referring to its column announcing criminal deeds and gaolbreaks).

There are several other interesting stones to be seen in All Saints Churchyard:

THOMAS THOMPSON, FARMER AT LOW HEATON DIED 23 DEC 1801 AGED 92

Thomas Thompson was blind, but according to his epitaph had an enormous amount of agricultural knowledge and skill.

REV. JOHN HARRIS DIED 6 NOVEMBER 1819

Rev Harris was a native of Reading in Berkshire. As well as being one of the first missionaries to the South Sea Islands, he was also a minister at Botany Bay. He finished his career at Hunstanworth in County Durham.

JANE, DAUGHTER OF JAMES FADDY AND SARAH SOPHIA HIS WIFE, DIED 10 JULY 1805 AGED 7 MONTHS

The broken headstone records the premature deaths of four other children in 1832, probably the result of the cholera epidemic that year.

THE FAMILY BURIAL PLACE OF MATTHEW ROBINSON, THOMAS HIS FATHER DIED 30 MARCH 1787

The anchor symbol on this stone may indicate 'hope' or a maritime connection.

ALL SAINTS CEMETERY

JESMOND ROAD

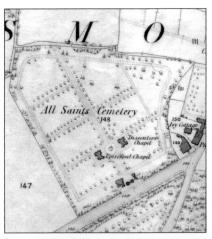

I n 1857 this municipal cemetery opened in rural Jesmond, some 20 years after the creation of the private Jesmond Old Cemetery on the opposite side of Jesmond Road. Large scale residential housing did not appear until later.

Benjamin Green, a noted Newcastle architect, designed the cemetery and its buildings including the fine Gothic arched gateway (illustrated), which contrasts sharply with John Dobson's neoclassical entrance across the road. Because the threat of grave robbers had passed by this time, cast iron railings with fleur-de-lys heads were considered adequate to enclose the area instead of the nine feet high stone wall which protected Jesmond Old Cemetery. Both chapels were set back on either side of a central carriageway which divided the cemetery into the Established Church to the west and nonconformists to the east. Only the western chapel is now in use for funerals. The east chapel operates as the Shrine Chapel of Our Lady of Jesmond and is open for services and private prayers at varying times during the week. The cemetery was extended to Osborne Avenue in the early 1900s, when land known as Dead Men's Graves was acquired. A pedestrian gate gives access to the enlarged cemetery. When Carliol Square Gaol was demolished in 1924 the bodies of executed criminals were transferred into unmarked graves in the cemetery. There have been nearly 90,000 burials here.

The map shows All Saints Cemetery in 1860. The east corner of Jesmond Old Cemetery is just across the road.

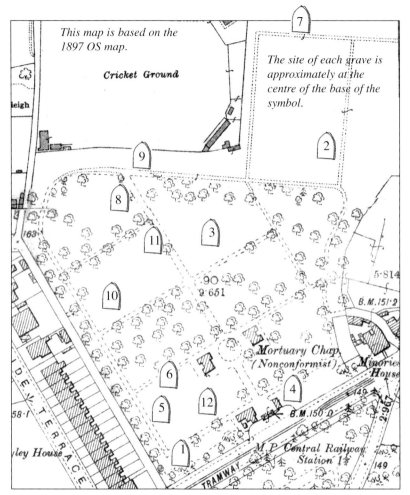

This map is based on the 1897 OS map.

Cricket Ground

The site of each grave is approximately at the centre of the base of the symbol.

Mortuary Chapel (Nonconformist)

1. Samuel Smith
2. Alexander Gardner
3. Michael Joseph Quigley
4. James Skinner
5. Francis Batey
6. George Richardson
7. Antonio Marcantonio
8. George Henry Carr
9. John James Lightfoot
10. Christopher John Bailey
11. Charles West Nichols
12. Josephine Esther Salisse

In unmarked graves are Thomas Harrison Hair and Catherine O'Hara.

WHO'S WHO IN ALL SAINTS CEMETERY

SAMUEL SMITH OBE JP (1872-1949) FOUNDER OF RINGTONS TEA

Born in Leeds, by the age of nine Sam was working as a butcher's boy on Friday nights and Saturdays to eke out his family's income. At 10 he left school to become an errand boy with one of Britain's best known tea merchants. Twenty-five years later, as a senior sales executive, he wanted to run his own business based on the door to door van delivery system working elsewhere in Yorkshire. His service agreement stopped him setting up his business in Yorkshire, so, despite having a family of six children under nine years of age, he moved to Newcastle where he set up in a small shop in Heaton with a partner called William Titterington. They called the company 'Ringtons'. Tea was imported direct from India and Sri Lanka, tasted, blended and packaged before delivery to customers in black, gold and green vans, initially drawn by well groomed horses. Up to 200 types of tea would be inspected and tasted each day, with the taster using pieces of apple to freshen his palate. The business prospered and moved into purpose-built premises in Algernon Road, Heaton in 1926.

Eventually there were 48 branches operating in the North.

Both World Wars brought setbacks, but the firm survived by diversifying into different products, as well as into coachbuilding which led to the formation of Smith's Electric Vehicles on Gateshead's Team Valley Trading Estate.

ALEXANDER GARDNER (1877-1921)
FOOTBALLER

Before the First World War, Newcastle United dominated the First Division of League football and attracted large crowds with their 'short passing game'. During a seven year period they won three league titles and appeared in four FA Cup finals (sadly winning only one of them).

For most of this time Alex captained the team at right half (midfielder today) and made 268 appearances scoring 20 goals. Alex came from Leith in 1899 and was one of six Scots in the 1904/05 team which won 23 out of 34 league games, as well as Newcastle's first league championship. A broken leg in 1909 ended Alex's footballing career and he became landlord of the Dun Cow Inn (now demolished) in Claremont Road.

Newcastle United v. Sunderland, 27 September 1904. Sunderland won 2-1.

MICHAEL JOSEPH QUIGLEY (1837-1924) AMERICAN CIVIL WAR VETERAN

Born in Bradford, Michael emigrated to America with his wife shortly before the outbreak of civil war. He served under General Robert E. Lee in Virginia but was wounded in his left arm, leaving his left hand virtually useless for the rest of his long life. He was later employed in Government Service, returning to the UK in 1876. He lived at St Lawrence Square off Walker Road, taking on various types of work. His income was subsidised by a pension from the American Government.

JAMES SKINNER (1836-1920) SHIPBUILDER

Born in London and educated in Scotland, he arrived on Tyneside, aged 14, to begin an apprenticeship at the former Coutts shipyard at Low Walker. Later he managed Andrew Leslie's shipyard at Hebburn for many years before opening a yard at Bill Quay with William Wood an ex shipyard cashier. This firm, Wood, Skinner & Co., successfully built 330 vessels, mainly small tramp coasters, trawlers and colliers, over a period of 42 years up to 1925. They also successfully built and launched an entire hospital! The 30-bed Tyne Floating Hospital for Infectious Diseases at Jarrow Slake, designed by Newcastle's Civil Engineer, George Laws, was launched on 2 August 1885 without breaking a single pane of glass. Accident prone, the hospital sank in 1888 but luckily nobody was aboard! She was refloated and stayed at her mooring for over 40 years.

FRANCIS BATEY (1841-1915) STEAM TUG BOAT OWNER

Francis joined his father's tug boat business at the age of 11 and eventually secured his master's certificate. When the Albert Edward Dock was opened by the Prince of Wales in 1884, he was assistant pilot on the *Rio Amazonas*, the first ship to enter the dock. He went on to be chairman of several Tyne Tug related companies and one of his sons, John Thomas Batey, became Managing Director of Hawthorn Leslie's Hebburn ship-yard.

GEORGE RICHARDSON (1797-1866) TIDE WAITER

Tide waiters were effectively customs officers who examined cargoes brought into port on the latest tide.

ANTONIO MARCANTONIO (MARK TONEY) (1886-1960) ICE CREAM MANUFACTURER

Courtesy Marcantonio Family

Antonio Marcantonio arrived in Newcastle, aged nine, to join a small colony of Italians living in Byker. It was as far north as their train fare would take them. In the early 1900s Antonio returned to Italy, briefly, to marry Angela before setting up home in Newcastle and beginning to make ice cream in a room in his house, using small pans of salt and ice to freeze it. Eventually he took over a small factory on Stepney bank, Ouseburn, and for many years made between 500 and 600 gallons of ice cream there daily. He also owned five ice cream parlours, the first one in the Grainger Arcade, and the business still flourishes.

GEORGE HENRY CARR (1867-1889) RACING CYCLIST

His 13ft monument features a shield on each side depicting a bicycle, flowers, the badge of the Jubilee Rovers Bicycle Club and the badge of Clarence Bicycle Club. He was a prominent figure on the racing circuit and died, aged 22, of inflammation of the brain (probably meningitis).

Founder members of the Ridley Cycling Club c.1891. The club was situated at the corner of Clarence Street and named after the Ridley pub. This photograph was taken at Blagdon because Lord Ridley took an interest in the club.

THOMAS HARRISON HAIR (1810-1875) ARTIST

Born in Newcastle, the son of a lamp black manufacturer and tanner, Hair worked in London and exhibited at the Royal Academy. He is probably best known for his *Views of the Collieries of Northumberland and Durham* and his work can be seen at Newcastle University's Hatton Gallery and the Laing Art Gallery. His grave is unmarked.

Laing Art Gallery

St Nicholas' Street c.1850 by Thomas Hair (detail).

JOHN JAMES LIGHTFOOT (1877-1897) APPRENTICE JOINER AND SANDGATE DISASTER VICTIM

John James was an apprentice joiner when he was killed, aged 19, crushed to death during restoration of a 200 year old two-storey beer-house, the Green Tree, in Robson's Entry, Sandgate. The building collapsed suddenly killing four and injuring 12 others. The disaster scene was sketched by the *Chronicle*'s artist and published on 6 March 1897,

the day after the accident. The article notes the consequences of the calamity: 'and in the

SCENE OF THE DISASTER: FROM A SKETCH BY OUR ARTIST.

house to the east there was a yawning space where the wall had tumbled in; behind the hole a staircase stood, but seemed, like the sword of Damocles, to have no more than a hair-strength to support it.' John James Lightfoot, the great-uncle of the author of this book, was unmarried.

CHRISTOPHER JOHN BAILEY (1861-1876)

Aged 15 years 11 months, he was killed by a fall from the main topmast, Cross Trees, of the barque *Araunah* off Cape Horn.

CHARLES WEST NICHOLS (1844-1869)

Drowned in the schooner *Blue Jacket* 19th October 1869. He and three friends went out on the schooner on the first part of her voyage, intending to return to shore with the tug. Suddenly a gale sprang up and they were unable to leave the ship. After three days on a turbulent sea, the *Blue Jacket* finally ran aground on the coast of Lincolnshire. There were no survivors.

JOSEPHINE ESTHER SALISSE (1905-1924)

From Thornton Heath, Surrey, Josephine died suddenly at her aunt's home in Stratford Road, Heaton, aged 19, and is remembered by a bronze female figure sorrowing over a sarcophagus.

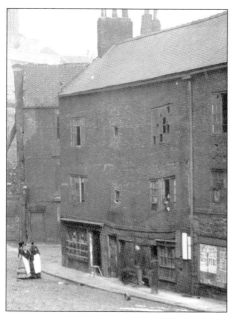

CATHERINE O'HARA (1787-1893)

She died at 106 at Tinners Entry, Wall Knoll. Born in Glasgow she brought up a large family and was a hawker of tapes, threads and needles. She spent her last years in poverty and lies in an unmarked grave.

Contrasting lives. Catherine O'Hara died in poverty near the Wall Knoll Tower (seen here c.1879) aged 106. She has no memorial.

St Andrew's Parish Church

Newgate Street

Newcastle's four parish churches have uncertain foundation dates but because St Andrew's Church has more of its 12th century masonry remaining than the others, it is often referred to as the oldest church. It first appears in records in 1218.

St Andrew's parish, Newcastle's most extensive, was not particularly wealthy, so its church was not elaborate. Recycled stones from the Roman Wall are visible in some of its lower courses. Originally there was no tower, and its high pitched roof dropped steeply over very narrow aisles to extremely low walls. A tower was added in the early 13th century. Other major improvements including widening the aisles, lengthening the chancel, adding transepts and a belfry, occurred later that century, probably due to compensation paid for the routing of the town wall through the churchyard.

During the Civil War period the tower served as a gun platform and suffered, as did the church generally, from enemy action. According to the parish register of 1644-45: 'ther was no child baptd. in this parish for 1 year's tim after the town was taken, nor sarmon in this church for 1 year's tim.' Also, because of Civil War damage, the church bells were silenced for over 80 years until, in 1726, new bells were cast. Bell ringing then continued until 1875 when it ceased because it was causing structural damage to the tower. Although still in place, the six bells (weighing over 53 tons) now chime electronically.

In 1707 stone flagging replaced trodden earth in the church and its aisles for the first time. More recently the floor of the nave and part of

St Andrew's church c.1723.

the chancel have been renewed with tiles and polished timber. Restoration work in the south transept by John Dobson (1844) revealed tombstones and the original piscina embedded in the walls.

Any number of local citizens wished to be buried within the church. These are a few of them:

1559: Humphrey Carr of Newcastle, yeoman 'directs that his body be buried in the parish church of St Andrew beside the bones of his mother.'

1573: Roger Resh of Newcastle, baker, 'directs that his body be buried in St Andrew's Church.' He left his belongings to various people: 'his chamlett jacket and a jacket of red russet ... his worst doublet and red russet gown, the fur of his best gown, his best cape, his best russet jacket and his best doublet.'

Wellbar House dwarfs St Andrew's Church in 2001.

1578: The will of John Thompson of St Andrew's parish stipulates that he 'desires to be buried in his parish church'. He left £6 13s 4d to an unmarried daughter and £3 6s 8d and his working gear with a pair of tenters (presumably for stretching cloth on hooks) to a son. After several other bequests 'he left 12d to the poor-man's box [and] to the repairing of some decayed places in the church way, 12d.'

1578: William Hall of Newcastle, cutler, 'directs that his body be buried in St Andrew's church'. His bequests included a cow to his wife, and to another person, 'his two best feather beds, two brass pots, three pewter plates, two pottle pots, four candlesticks, best table, two chests and the chimneys in the hall.'

1578: John Bird of Newcastle 'desires to be buried in St Andrew's church, as near his father as may be'. He bequeathed to his son 'an iron chimney, a feather bed, a bolster, a coverlet, two codds and a pair of linen sheets.'

1646: 'Hugh Brown, buried in the church, the King's (Charles I) Kouchman'.

Who's who in St Andrew's church

In the floor of Trinity Chapel (underneath a carpet) lies the 14th century family vault belonging to Sir Adam de Athol. He originated from Ponteland, and, according to tradition, he gave the Town Moor to the Burgesses of Newcastle. The large inscribed memorial brass which once covered the ledger stone was removed for safekeeping a long time ago. The outline of Sir Adam, dressed in armour, together with sword and dagger, can still be made out on the tombstone.

Sir Adam's feet, resting on a leopard, from the now-vanished brass.

Other interments in Trinity Chapel include some of the occupiers of 'Alderman Fenwick's House' on Pilgrim Street Newcastle:

Nicholas Fenwick, merchant adventurer, who died in 1725 aged 62 – the family home in Pilgrim Street became a coaching inn, then a liberal club and today this Grade I listed building contains offices.

Thomas Winship, tanner, and his wife Jane were the parents of Sarah, wife of Nicholas Fenwick, and to whom the Pilgrim Street House originally belonged.

Christopher Rutter, baker and brewer, who occupied part of Fenwick's Pilgrim Street premises for his business.

Alderman Fenwick's House, Pilgrim Street c.1723.

There is also a 13th century cross slab featuring a plain incised cross with mason's or carpenter's square. It is probably in memory of someone who had worked on the church building.

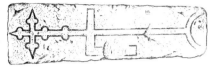

Beneath the 19th century organ are several more burials including that of:

WILLIAM NEWTON (1730-1798) BUILDER, ARCHITECT

Newton was Newcastle's leading architect in the mid-to late-18th century. The son of a Newcastle shipwright, he was baptised at St Andrew's Church. He designed St Ann's Church, City Road, in 1768, his first substantial commission. He also planned Charlotte Square (from 1769) and lived there for about 20 years. In 1776 he designed the Assembly Rooms, Westgate Street. His commissions outside Newcastle included Backworth Hall, Castle Eden Hall and Howick Hall. He married Dorothy Bell of Gateshead and they had twelve children.

CUTHBERT LAMBERT (1701-1772) SURGEON

Lambert's Leap.

In the chancel, among other well-worn ledger stones, is the last resting place of local surgeon Cuthbert Lambert and some of his family. The stone is now probably under the tiled floor. Lambert was the son of a Hexham surgeon who practised in Pilgrim Street for nearly 50 years. His son, Cuthbert Lambert (1743-1770) at 16 survived a horrific accident at Sandyford bridge, when his horse suddenly bolted and failed to take an awkward bend – the horse plunged to its death into the ravine while young Lambert avoided serious injury by clinging to a tree – a commemorative stone (dated 1759) marks the scene today at Lambert's Leap, Sandyford Road. He too was buried here aged 27.

Also in the chancel is a 15th century grave cover which depicts three horse shoes and a hammer. It probably commemorates a farrier and bears a Latin inscription asking for prayers for the soul of Thomas Lytton.

For many years this stone stood in the churchyard.

Another visible stone in the chancel is to William Reed, a former gaoler at Newgate prison, who died in 1683. Gaolers are said to have lived in a substantial house, opposite the church in Newgate Street, taken over by Bourgognes as a wine house about 1876.

ST ANDREW'S CHURCHYARD

The churchyard was reduced in area around 1280 to accommodate the building of the town wall which helped preserve the church in those early and lawless times. More recently the church and churchyard have protected this part of the town wall and enabled it to survive.

St Andrew's c.1900.

In 1377 the Bishop of Durham authorised the chaplains of the church 'to erect honest buildings in the churchyard and to apply the rents and profits to the uses of the chapel' while reserving ample space for burials. At this period the church seems to have had difficulty balancing its financial accounts.

In 1783 'Parishioners purchased a piece of waste ground, lying on the west side of the churchyard, to enlarge their burial ground.' It took the vicar three years to get the bishop to consecrate the land, meanwhile the churchyard was becoming more and more overcrowded.

Newcastle Corporation allowed the parish to take down part of the town wall in 1818, including the Andrew Tower, between the north-west corner of the church tower and St Andrew Street (Darn Crook). The vault of the Andrew Tower had been used for many years as a charnel house. The churchyard was extended into an adjoining part of the King's Dykes and enclosed with a wall topped by iron railings. By 1825 the area of churchyard, excluding the church, measured 4,342 square yards (nearly an acre).

The widening of Gallowgate in 1895 reduced the area of the churchyard by 220 square

yards (about five per cent) – the disturbed human remains together with 14 stones were re-interred in St Andrew's Cemetery on Tankerville Terrace, though some of these memorial stones are now missing. Many people, including the vicar of St Andrew's who led the protest, were concerned about the possible spread of cholera from exhumed victims. These objections were dismissed by the city's medical officer.

The churchyard area had been reduced in the 1780s when a vestry was built on the north side of the chancel. It was replaced in 1904-5 by the present two storey vestry. A new Parish Hall opened in 1960 occupying even more of the shrinking churchyard. In 1907, 327 grave-stones were recorded in the churchyard. Interestingly a 'squint' remains visible on the inside of the chancel north wall which, it is said, was to enable lepers to view the altar from outside the church before the first vestry was built.

Cut into an end of the Town Wall near the church tower are several carvings resembling musical notes. They probably refer to grave markers and may well have contained metal plates, suitably engraved or numbered, relating to the reservation of grave plots.

WHO'S WHO IN ST ANDREW'S CHURCHYARD

For several centuries the adjacent Newgate was the town gaol. Prisoners sentenced to be hanged were led to the gallows outside the town walls (near the Regional Blood Transfusion Centre at Fenham). They were usually buried in St Andrew's churchyard on the north (unconsecrated) side. The county gaol was at the castle with executions taking place there or outside the Westgate, and burials at St John's churchyard.

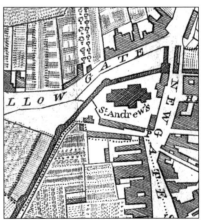

St Andrew's and the town wall in 1788. The map was engraved by Ralph Beilby.

Witchcraft hysteria reached its climax in 17th century Europe and many towns employed a witchfinder. Newcastle was no exception. A witchfinder was hired from Scotland on the basis of 20 shillings (£1) for each person convicted, plus travelling expenses, at a time when labourers earned about a shilling a day. A witch was not supposed to bleed when pricked with a pin or needle, but many professional witchfinders used retractable needles which would not pierce the skin. In 1650 14 witches and a wizard from Newcastle were hanged at Gallowgate and buried at St Andrew's churchyard in unmarked graves. Some sources add that to prevent the witches attempting to walk after death iron bolts were fixed into their knee joints. The witchfinder con-

tinued his business elsewhere but was finally caught in Scotland where, just before his hanging he confessed to causing the deaths of over 220 women in England and Scotland.

In 1765 the sexton of St Andrew's Church, was found dead in a grave which he had been digging.

James O'Neil was executed on the Town Moor, Newcastle in 1816. He had robbed Mr George Angus, a carrier from Mickley, on the highway as he was returning from the Cow-Hill fair, the previous October. When the body was cut down, friends of O'Neil took it to a public house near the gaol for a wake. On the following day, Sunday, O'Neil was interred at St Andrews churchyard. About 30 Irish people attended the funeral.

JOHN GRAHAM CLARKE (1735-1818) COAL OWNER AND MERCHANT TRADING WITH THE WEST INDIES

John Graham Clarke was the grandfather of Elizabeth Barrett Browning, the poetess. His daughter, Mary Clarke, married Edward Moulton Barrett at St Nicholas' Church, South Gosforth, (another family of Merchants trading with the West Indies) and their daughter Elizabeth eloped with poet Robert Browning in 1846. His worn ledger stone lies in the path.

John Graham Clarke and wife Arabella lived initially at Pilgrim Street on the site of the old Odeon Cinema then at Kenton Lodge (the original building at the corner of Grandstand Road and Kenton Road is now demolished) and finally at Fenham Hall, where they both died.

CHARLES AVISON (1709-1770) COMPOSER, CONDUCTOR AND ORGANIST

Charles Avison was born in Newcastle, the son of a town 'wait' (musician) who played in the town band. His mother was probably a church organist. Charles became an outstanding figure in the musical life of 18th century Newcastle and arguably the most important English concerto composer of the 18th century. He organised subscription concerts at the Groat Market Assembly Rooms and also held benefit concerts for the Infirmary. He was church organist at St Nicholas' for 34 years at a salary of £50 a year for most of this time and supplemented his income by teaching. Avison's orchestra at various times included some well known names: William Herschel the astronomer, William Shield, Master of the King's Music and a pupil of Avison, and Ralph Beilby (double bass), the famous engraver. In addition to the tombstone (renewed in 1890 by public subscription) a commemorative plaque exists on the churchyard wall in Newgate Street erected by the Avison Society.

RALPH BEILBY (1743-1817) SILVERSMITH, JEWELLER AND ENGRAVER

Born in Durham city, the son of a silversmith and jeweller, Ralph Beilby was the business brain of his family and when the business failed in Durham he instigated the move to Tyneside. Proficient in the classics, art and music, Beilby sponsored popular

The tall house (centre left) is Beilby's workshop at Amen Corner.

musical evenings and was a founder member of Newcastle's Literary and Philosophical Society. Music, drawing, engraving and enamelling were all represented in the talented family. Beilby took on Thomas Bewick as an apprentice engraver at the age of 14 in 1767, and encouraged him in the wood engraving side of the business which Beilby disliked. Thomas was an 'unruly lad', so Ralph imposed a 7pm curfew and insisted he read the Bible each evening to old Mrs Beilby. Later, Ralph and Thomas entered into partnership and carried on their engraving business at Amen Corner, Newcastle, for over 20 years until a disagreement forced them to part company in 1797.

Ralph excelled in 'ornamented silver engraving' and was reckoned 'one of the best in the Kingdom' while Thomas Bewick became famous for his wood engraving of birds and animals.

Thomas Bewick.

WILLIAM CHAPMAN (1750-1832) INVENTOR OF THE COAL DROP

Born at Whitby, William Chapman was the son of an inventive sea captain who is credited with a method of making salt water fresh (c1758). By the age of 18 he was captain of a merchant vessel and he then trained to be a civil engineer. He became resident engineer to the County of Kildare Canal, consulting engineer to the Grand Canal of Ireland, and invented the skew arch. He was also involved in the survey of a proposed canal from Newcastle to the Irish Sea in 1795. Among his inventions was the 'coal drop' (above) patented c.1800.

William Chapman.

It amounted to a substantial timber construction at the riverside which lowered loaded coal wagons into sailing vessels, solving the problem of 'broken' coal. Chapman's tombstone is now missing but a mural monument to his memory exists in the chancel of the church.

LUKE CLENNELL (1781-1840) ARTIST

Born at Ulgham, near Morpeth, into a farming family, Clennell was apprenticed aged 16 to Thomas Bewick to become a wood engraver. He turned out to be a most gifted pupil. He went to London in his mid-twenties, winning a gold palette and a gold medal for his engravings.

Marriage to Elizabeth Warren, the daughter of a well-known engraver, led him to meet other artists and his eventual decision to become a painter. He received many commissions and his oil-sketch *The Charge of the Life Guards at Waterloo* won him a prize of 150 guineas. Anxiety over an offer of 1,500 guineas to paint a huge group portrait of nearly 400 'Allied Sovereigns and their Generals' at a banquet in 1814 at London's Guildhall pushed him towards insanity and into a London mental home in 1817. He was only 36. Tragically his wife died soon afterwards and

One of Clennell's apprenticeship engravings for Thomas Bewick.

Clennell never recovered. The last 13 years of his life were spent back in North East England, mostly as an inmate of Newcastle's lunatic asylum on Bath Lane, where he died. Although buried in the churchyard in an unmarked grave, his friends later subscribed to a marble tablet, with painter's palette, now fixed to the chancel wall (illustrated above).

JAMES ARCHBOLD (1781-1849) SLATER, TILER AND LIMEBURNER

The son of a Gallowgate slater, James Archbold became a wealthy businessman and property owner in Newcastle. Archbold Terrace, Jesmond, is named after him. He was a Newcastle coun-

cillor, then Sheriff (1840), and finally Mayor (1846) Alderman and JP. Though a rich man he continued to live at his place of business, nearly opposite Darn Crook, and couldn't be persuaded to live in better surroundings as a local rhyme commented:

I' the toon of Newcassel James Archbold dis dwell,
He's a slater te trade, and thinks ne small beer on
hissel;
And in Gallowgate, just aside the Darn Crook,
Stands his house amang smells that wad make a horse puke.

There are monuments to Archbold in the chancel of St Andrew's and the nave of St Nicholas.

THE FAMILY VAULT OF AUBONE SURTEES (1777-1859) WINE AND SPIRITS IMPORTER, AND HOSTMAN

The tombstone in the path outside the south porch of the church covers the family vault of Aubone Surtees No. 3, the grandson of the first Aubone Surtees and nephew of Bessie Surtees whose famous elopement down a ladder from the family house on Sandhill in 1771 with John Scott (later Lord Eldon) so shocked the family at the time.

Aubone himself is not interred here because he died after the churchyard's closure in 1854. He lies in Jesmond Old Cemetery together with his wife and some of his family. However, four of his 14 children are buried here including William Aubone Surtees who, at 35, died from a fall in the billiard room of Newcastle Cricket Ground.

MARY TURNER (1760-1797) FIRST WIFE OF THE REVEREND WILLIAM TURNER

Mary was the first wife of the Rev. William Turner (1762-1859), Unitarian Minister at the Hanover Square Chapel for 59 years, and schoolmaster. He was instrumental in founding the Literary and Philosophical Society of Newcastle in 1793 and was its secretary for the first 44 years. He delivered about 600 lectures there over a 30 year period on topics ranging from electricity to astronomy.

Mary was also the cousin of Mrs Gaskell

Rev. William Turner.

the author, who, before her marriage, spent some time with the Turners at their home in what is now Westgate Road. Mrs Gaskell's controversial novel *Ruth* was based on her experiences in Newcastle, with some of its characters founded on the Turner household. Mary is buried with two of her infant children.

The grave also contains William Turner's second wife Jane (née Willits) (1758-1826). She was the daughter of a Midlands vicar, a niece of Josiah Wedgewood the pottery manufacturer, and related to his first wife's family, the Hollands.

JANE SMITH (1737-1820) STEP-DAUGHTER OF JOHN WESLEY (1703-1791)

At 47 John Wesley, the founder of Methodism, married Mary (Molly) Vazeille, a bad tempered but wealthy London widow. Later, Jane Vazeille, one of her four children, wedded William Smith, a Newcastle corn merchant, a prominent local Methodist and the constant companion of John Wesley whenever he visited Tyneside. During these visits Jane Smith made every effort to comfort her stepfather, realising he was the subject of intolerable behaviour from her mother. On one occasion Molly dragged her husband by his hair around the floor. Jane and other members of her immediate family are buried here though John and Molly Wesley are interred in London.

RICHARD SWARLEY (1739-1807) PUBLICAN

Swarley was proprietor of the Black Boy Inn, Groat Market, where the enterprising publican encouraged Newcastle's tradesmen to meet for pleasant evenings and discussion of topical issues such as the American War of Independence. They became known as Swarley's Club and Thomas Bewick was probably the best-known member – his membership card calls it 'The Newcastle House of Lords'. Any bad behaviour resulted in a fine or expulsion and meetings ended no later than 10pm.

Swarley's very worn gravestone lies in the pathway, and his best memorial, the old Blackie Boy Inn, with its upstairs meeting room, can still be visited in the Groat Market.

The Black Boy Inn is on the right of this view of the Groat Market.

ST ANDREW'S CEMETERY

TANKERVILLE TERRACE, JESMOND

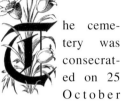

The cemetery was consecrated on 25 October 1858, the same day as St John's Cemetery, Elswick. It occupies a ten acre site at Moor Edge near Brandling Place, Jesmond.

At that time there was no housing in this area of Jesmond and the railway line had not yet been constructed. The approach to the cemetery was from the Great North Road as Tankerville Terrace had not yet been built. There have been just over 43,000 burials here to date. Both chapels are now disused.

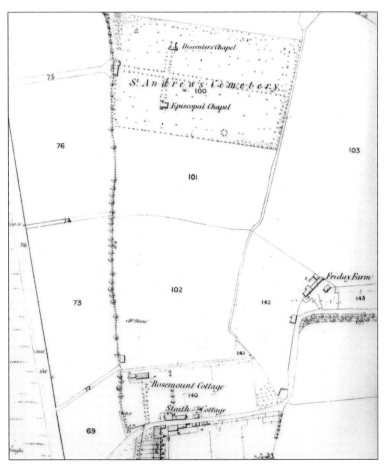

The brand new St Andrew's Cemetery as shown on the First Edition OS map, 1860. The Great North Road is on the left. The long forgotten Friday Farm is now submerged beneath suburban streets and the Metro railway line.

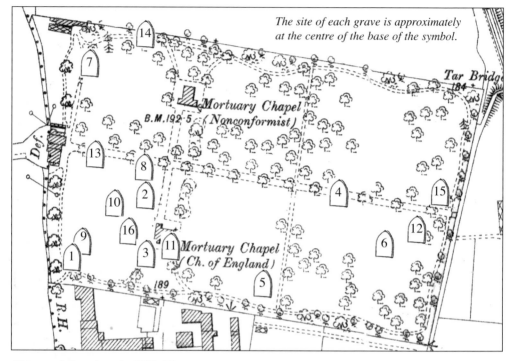

This map is based on the 1897 OS map.

1. Gustavo Barawitzka
2. Eileen Maud Blair
3. Edward Brough
4. William Edward Curtis
5. Dr Dennis Embleton
6. John Burghersh Forbes
7. Sir Claude Dixon Gibb
8. John Hall
9. Dr Thomas Emerson Headlam
10. Ralph Hedley
11. Drs G.H. and W.E. Hume

12. Sir George Burton Hunter
13. William Lister Newcombe
14. Police Constable Bain
15. John McKay
16. John Pritchard

In an unmarked grave is Zaza Ben-I-Ford

WHO'S WHO IN ST ANDREW'S CEMETERY

GUSTAVO BARAWITZKA (1856-1936) PROPRIETOR OF THE CRITERION RESTAURANT

Gustavo Barawitzka, a well known figure in Newcastle, was founder and proprietor of the Criterion Restaurant in Market Street which catered for Newcastle businessmen for many years.

Gustavo arrived on Tyneside from Italy aged 18 in the mid-1870s and obtained British nationality in 1901. Ten years earlier a banquet, organised by the local Italian community in Newcastle, had been held in the Criterion Restaurant to commemorate the 21st anniversary of the storming of Rome which led to the unification of Italy. During the after dinner speeches, local politician and businessman Joseph Cowen was referred to as 'The greatest English friend Italy had ever possessed'.

Gustavo's impressive mausoleum, in the 'classical' style, stands in the south-west corner of the cemetery.

Market Street in 1928. The Criterion was on the right near the junction with Pilgrim Street.

Eileen Maud Blair (1905-1945) First wife of George Orwell

The daughter of a customs collector, Eileen O'Shaughnessy was born in South Shields and attended Sunderland High School before going on to Oxford University. She later managed a typing bureau.

George Orwell (real name Eric Arthur Blair), the English essayist, journalist and novelist, married Eileen when he was sent by the socialist Left Book Club to northern England in 1936 to study the unemployment situation.

During the second world war Eileen produced the BBC radio programme *The Kitchen Front* which dealt mainly with recipes and ways to eke out available rations. By now her husband was a BBC war correspondent for the *Indian Service*. They adopted a son from among the unwanted wartime babies (pictured above with Eileen Blair). In 1945 Eileen died of a heart attack following a routine operation at a private clinic in Fernwood House, Clayton Road, Jesmond (formerly the home of Sir Walter Runciman the ship

owner). In *Animal Farm* Orwell credited Eileen with helping to plan the book and 'adding vital sparks of humour'. His other celebrated work *1984* draws partly on her wartime experiences while employed at the Ministry of Food.

Orwell lived for another five years, working between the remote island of Jura and London where he died of tuberculosis in 1950 aged 47.

Edward Brough (1846-1933) Grocer and benefactor

Born in America, Edward was brought to Tyneside by his family aged two. When he grew up he worked for a local firm of provision importers and then in partnership in a wholesale provision business importing mainly butter and eggs.

At the age of 42, Edward and his eldest son John William set up their own wholesale provi-

sion business with a shop in Farrington Court, Bigg Market. John William, aged 23, then branched out on his own into retailing, eventually to be followed by his father. Their shop in Blackett Street and subsequent premises had no window display merely a prominent sign 'Wholesale Cash Store'. The policy of cash on deliv-

One of Brough's Stores, 1912.

ery guaranteed no bad debts. They bought in bulk, cut out the middleman and so were able to reduce prices to the consumer. Later, travelling salesmen were employed to secure distant customers' orders and provide an efficient delivery system. The business proved successful and at one time had over 500 employees. It sold out to the Meadow Dairy Co Ltd in 1919.

The Broughs were generous to local charities and in particular to the Poor Children's Holiday Association. They donated a house in Whickham to be used as the 'Edith Brough Children's Home'. Edward made various charitable bequests in his will, as well as leaving one year's wages to each of his indoor and outdoor employees who were in employment for at least a year before his death.

WILLIAM EDWARD CURTIS (1889-1969) PHYSICIST

William E. Curtis was Professor of Physics at Newcastle University for nearly 30 years from 1926. He was one of Britain's chief atomic research pioneers, a Fellow of the Royal Society, and in 1962 was awarded the CBE for services to education.

The public lecture theatre in the Herschel Building at Newcastle University was named the Curtis Auditorium in his memory.

DR DENNIS EMBLETON (1810-1900) PHYSICIAN

Dennis was born in Newcastle, the son of an inn keeper. He was physician to the Newcastle Infirmary 1853-1878 and the first Professor of Medicine in Newcastle. Dr Embleton's dispenser at the Forth Infirmary was James Crossley Eno. Dr Embleton reputedly gave Eno a recipe for a laxative drink that became known as 'Eno's Fruit Salts'.

JOHN BURGHERSH FORBES (1819-1895) HERO OF BALACLAVA

A native of Scotland, Forbes joined the 4th Light Dragoons (later the 4th Hussars) at an early age. At the age of 35 he was fighting in the Crimean War and was slightly wounded during the ill-fated charge of the Light Brigade in 1854 in their attempt to silence the Russian guns on the heights of Balaclava. Forbes was taken prisoner during the 20-minute encounter in which over half of the Brigade were either killed or badly wounded.

Following his discharge from the army, Forbes became Regimental Sergeant Major of the Northumberland Hussars and for the last 25 years of his life was Riding Master at the Riding School on Northumberland Road, where he also lived. This classical style brick building, designed in 1847 by John Dobson, is today used by Northumbria University.

Twice married, with a family of six children, Forbes received a full military funeral with his oak coffin carried on a gun carriage covered with the Union Jack and drawn by six horses.

From Ward's Directory 1881-82.

THE ART OF RIDING

TAUGHT AT THE RIDING SCHOOL,

Bath Road, Northumberland St., Newcastle,

BY

J. B. FORBES,

Sergeant-Major Northumberland Hussars, late Troop Sergeant-Major
Fourth (Queen's Own) Hussars.

CARDS OF TERMS MAY BE HAD AT THE RIDING SCHOOL.

Sir Claude Dixon Gibb (1898-1959) FRS Industrialist

An Australian by birth, Gibb served as a pilot in France during World War I. In 1924 he began a 35 year association with C.A. Parsons & Co. at their Heaton Works, Newcastle, rising from electrical engineering apprentice to Chairman and Managing Director. He proposed the application of atomic energy to generate electric power and Parsons supplied the turbo alternators for the UK's first nuclear power station at Calder Hall in Cumbria in 1954. Gibb was knighted in 1945 and awarded the FRS in 1946. A hall of residence at Northumbria University is named after him.

John Hall (1824-1899) Ship Owner and philanthropist

Born in Pilgrim Street, Newcastle above his father's carver and gilder's shop, John, one of six

children, attended the Royal Grammar School before working as an office boy on the Quayside.

At 27 John set up as a merchant and ship owner. His business interests expanded and he even acquired a large wooded estate in Sweden from which he imported timber. He formed a partnership with his brother James which traded from premises at the Royal Arcade. Their business was well respected with high trading standards both for personnel and for cargoes. The Hall brothers ensured their ships were safe to sail in, and not the 'floating coffins' used by some entrepreneurs. They were said to be the first Tyneside ship owners to switch from sail to steam.

John, who never married, was a life long philanthropist. In 1897 there were plans to rebuild the Infirmary at the Forth in celebration of Queen Victoria's diamond jubilee and £100,000 had already been raised. John thought the Forth was an unsuitable area (see page 163) and offered another £100,000 provided the next infirmary was built at Castle Leazes, which is where the Royal Victoria Infirmary was constructed.

John died at 3 Ellison Place. His oak coffin was made of wood from the old belfry of St Nicholas' Cathedral and a window in the south aisle of the chancel of St Nicholas' is dedicated to his memory. His father, mother, brother James and his wife are also interred in his vault.

DR THOMAS EMERSON HEADLAM (1777-1864) PHYSICIAN AND WHIG POLITICIAN

The youngest son of the Tyne's leading shipbuilder at that time, based at South Shore Gateshead, Thomas attended Newcastle's Royal Grammar School. He studied at Edinburgh University and graduated in medicine in 1800.

He married Isabella the eldest daughter of Sir William Loraine of Kirkharle. They lived in Charlotte Square, then in Northumberland Street, and also had a country retreat in what is now Jesmond Dene, initially at Crag Hall and then at Black Dene House (now rebuilt as Jesmond Dene House). Dene Bridge between Castles Farm and Craghall bears his initials and the date 1850. His only child, Charles, was Newcastle's postmaster for many years.

For over 50 years Thomas was Newcastle's leading physician, becoming Newcastle's most prominent public figure during the first half of the 19th century, and a familiar face at the Infirmary (see page 163). His obituary in *The Lancet* referred to him as 'one of the most eminent English provincial physicians'. He was a key figure in founding the College of Medicine in 1851.

As a dedicated Whig, he supported political reform under Earl Grey. Following municipal reform in 1835 he became a councillor for St Andrew's Ward, then an Alderman and JP. He served twice as Mayor of Newcastle (in 1837 and 1845). For many years he was Vice President of the Literary and Philosophical Society and served as its President for five years.

At his funeral huge crowds lined the route to the cemetery from his son's house in Ridley Place. Headlam Street in Byker is named in his memory.

RALPH HEDLEY (1848-1913) ARTIST
AND WOOD ENGRAVER

Ralph's father, an itinerant joiner from North Yorkshire, realised his son's artistic talent at an early age, but sensibly insisted he should have a trade because of the unpredictability of the art world.

Ralph served an apprenticeship as a wood carver. He earned eightpence for a 12 hour day, which began at 6am. Later he set up as an 'Artistic & Architectural Carver' in New Bridge Street, where he was prepared to tackle any job. His versatility extended to making models and moulds for Joseph Swan's new and innovative light bulb and he is supposed to have suggested to Swan the familiar pear shaped light bulb we use today. Church furnishings were the backbone of his business, and there are few Tyneside churches without some of his carvings. St Nicholas' Church in Newcastle was upgraded to cathedral status in 1882 and much of the refurbishment, including the Bishop's throne, was produced by Ralph. The angels along the side of the choir are said to have been modelled on Ralph's thirteen-year-old daughter.

As a boy, Ralph had some evening tuition from William Bell Scott at the Newcastle School of Art. Once his wood carving business was well established he began painting for the rising group of wealthy local business men. His special talent lay in the interpretation of working people, in particular children, and domestic animals. Some of his best work includes *The Ballad Seller, The News-Boy, Going Home* (illustrated) and *Geordie ha'ad the Bairn*. For 15 years he regularly exhibited up to five paintings at the Royal Academy.

Ralph's younger days were spent at Elswick. After his marriage, he lived successively at Shieldfield, Jesmond Dene Terrace and Belle Grove Terrace, Spital Tongues. He had five children.

Laing Art Gallery

'Going Home' by Ralph Hedley.

Dr George Haliburton Hume (1846-1923) Surgeon
Dr William Errington Hume (1879-1960) Physician

Two generations of the well known Hume family are interred here. There were plans to bury grandson George (Cardinal Basil Hume) here too, but it was considered more appropriate for him to lie in Westminster Cathedral in London among other RC Cardinals and Archbishops.

Dr William Errington.

The Hume family originated in the Scottish borders where they farmed land around Kelso. William married Elizabeth Haliburton and one of their sons, George Haliburton, studied medicine at Edinburgh University, qualifying as a surgeon at the age of 20. For many years he acted as surgeon at Newcastle's Infirmary and lived nearby at Westgate Road. In 1881 he moved to 4 Ellison Place.

His son William Errington (1879-1960) born at Westgate Road, was one of five children. He studied medicine at Cambridge then returned to Newcastle to specialise in cardiology at the RVI. During the first world war, he volunteered to serve in France, where he was able to study, among other problems, the effects of poison gas and how to combat wet trench disease. He was mentioned in despatches and awarded the CMG. He also met his future wife, Marie, in France.

After the war, they returned to Newcastle, and their five children were born at Ellison Place where William practised. He introduced the electrocardiograph to Newcastle and received a knighthood in 1952 for services to medicine. Later in life, William suffered osteoarthritis, which restricted his passion for fishing, but led him to become an expert embroiderer. The children became fluent in French. Marie encouraged George (later Basil) to become a priest. He eventually became head of the Roman Catholic Church in Britain.

A ward at the Royal Victoria Infirmary c.1930.

Sir George Burton Hunter (1845-1937) Shipbuilder and Philanthropist

Not many eight-year-old boys have the opportunity to sail around the world. However, as the son of a Sunderland ship owner and sea captain, George Burton Hunter was able to make the trip. He had a few years of formal schooling then, at the age of 13, began an engineering apprenticeship. By the age of 20 he was in charge of a drawing office.

A workaholic, and largely self taught, he was head hunted in his mid thirties by the Swan family after the tragic death of Charles Sheriton Swan, who is buried at Longbenton. He immediately resigned his shipbuilding partnership of Austin and Hunter on Wearside, to form a new firm at Walker, with the widow of C.S. Swan, which became known as C.S. Swan & Hunter.

In 1903, Hunter organised the merger with another Tyneside shipyard, J. Wigham Richardson, to form Swan Hunter and Wigham Richardson Ltd, with a view to bid for the contract to build the world's largest luxury liner for Cunard. About 6,000 men worked on *Mauretania*, which was launched in 1906. A major innovation devised by Hunter was the glazed roof building berth, which protected workers in bad weather.

Hunter married Ann Hudson, niece of George Hudson MP, the 'Railway King' and they had five children. For several years they lived at Wallsend, before settling at Clayton Road, Jesmond, around 1890. Hunter gave land for St Luke's Church, Wallsend, and its vicarage. In 1914, he bought Wallsend Hall and its surrounding grounds and then gifted them two years later to the Borough for civic use. Today the building is the Civic Hall. The Sir G.B. Hunter Memorial Hospital is in adjacent buildings. In

Mauretania on the stocks at Swan Hunter, 1906.

1918 Hunter received a knighthood for services rendered during World War I.

William Lister Newcombe (1848-1929) Architect

Born in Gateshead, the son of a Newcastle businessman, and educated at Dr Bruce's Academy in Percy Street, he went on to become one of Newcastle's leading architects. Perhaps his best known design was for the Royal Victoria Infirmary, jointly with H.P. Adams. The imposing classical style monument over his grave is attractively designed in sandstone ashlar with four Tuscan columns, wreaths and a Greek inscription. The adjacent chest tomb belongs to his parents, Frederick and Ann Newcombe, with the nearby red granite coped stone covering the grave of his brother, Frederick William Newcombe, MD JP, and wife Emily.

The RVI in 1912 from across the lake in Leazes Park.

PC Bain (1826-1867) 'Killed by an explosion of nitroglycerine on the Town Moor 17th December 1867, while in the execution of his duty'

The nitroglycerine (used in mines for blasting) had spent several months in a cellar at the White Swan Inn Yard in the Cloth Market. It was far too dangerous to be stored in such a busy part of town so a magistrate's warrant was issued for its removal. John Mawson, the town's newly-elected Sheriff, who was a chemist by trade, was asked for advice on the best way to dispose of the explosive. He recommended that they pour the liq-

uid down a disused mine shaft on the Town Moor. A party of seven, including Mawson, Thomas Bryson, the town surveyor, and PC Bain set off to tackle the problem. After six canisters of the oily green liquid had been poured away, it was discovered that the contents of the other three had crystallised. While they were discussing how to deal with this new problem, there was a tremendous explosion. Contemporary sources reported 'pieces of flesh and limbs torn from their sockets lying scattered about' and the noise of the explosion being heard up to fifteen miles away. Five of the party, including PC Bain, died instantly. Mawson and Bryson were blinded and deafened and both died two days later. Mawson and Bryson are buried in Jesmond Old Cemetery.

ZAZA BEN-I-FORD (1901-1929) ALGERIAN DANCER

One of the attractions of the North East Coast Exhibition in 1929, held on part of Newcastle's Town Moor, was an African mud-hut village where natives were to live for six months in front of thousands of inquisitive visitors daily.

Primarily the Exhibition was of an industrial nature intended to revive a sagging North East economy, but it was also meant to educate, entertain and amuse (see illustration over page).

Although the Exhibition was a financial success (as well as seeing the birth of Exhibition Ale, Smith's Crisps and a child in the African Village), it also suffered a tragedy. A 28-year-old Algerian dancer, unable to cope with the Tyneside summer

Algerian dancers arrive at King's Cross station on their way to the North East Coast Exhibition, May 1929.

climate, died in Walkergate Hospital from a chill apparently caught on the journey to England. She was given a full Muslim funeral at the grave side, attended by about 50 mourners, including her husband. Sadly her eight-month-old baby was left motherless. At the moment the grave is unmarked, but plans are afoot to commission a headstone from an Algerian stonemason.

The North East Coast Exhibition attracted millions over the summer of 1929.

JOHN McKAY (1884-1964) MINER, MP AND HONORARY FREEMAN OF WALLSEND

John McKay was already a miner by the time he was 12 in 1896, but in 1910 he became the first miner to gain a diploma in economics and political science from Ruskin College, Oxford. He became MP for Wallsend in 1945.

JOHN PRITCHARD (1830-1868) TRAGEDIAN

All we know about John Pritchard is what he looked like and that he must have been an actor – presumably specialising in tragedy – and a Freemason. The carvings on his striking gravestone (right) depict theatrical masks and masonic symbols. The cemetery architect was named 'Pritchard of Darlington' – could there be any connection?

St Paul's Church and Chapel

Arthur's Hill, Westgate

In 1841 the vicar of St John's Church in Newcastle opened a new church at his own expense, at Arthur's Hill, opposite Westgate Hill Cemetery. He believed this two-storey building, seating 700, would become the parish church of the proposed new district of St Paul's. The vicar, Reverend William Wright, was a brother-in-law of Richard Grainger the Newcastle property developer.

The chapel c.1900, and, below, all that remains of the churchyard memorial stones today.

It was an expensive gamble as Wright later found he could not sell the new church on to the Church Commissioners as planned and, unable to afford the mortgage, was forced to sell at auction. The Independents (later Congregationalists) met the reserve price of £1,600 and the chapel opened for worship in 1855. Some tokens of Anglican worship, such as the Royal Arms and font, remained in the church but the external cross was chiselled off and buried in the churchyard. A new parish church, dedicated to St Paul, and designed by Benjamin Green, opened nearby in Havelock Street in 1854.

Often described as the plague cemetery, this was not Newcastle's only burial ground for the 1,533 known cholera victims of the 1853 outbreak. At this time it was a normal parish churchyard and as such took its share of the town's deaths (about 340) virtually all within a period of approximately four weeks. (For a map of the graveyard see page 100.)

Some years after the closure of urban churchyards in 1854, at which time it is estimated over 2200 burials had taken place, the graveyard was converted into a recreation area known as

the Dotchin Garden of Rest. John Anderson Dotchin, a Newcastle ironmonger, had long been actively connected with St Paul's Congregational Church. You can still see several headstones lined up against the north wall of the recreation area.

The chapel became a recreation centre for the unemployed in 1931 before opening as the Gem Cinema three years later. In 1967 the cinema was demolished and the site is now a car park.

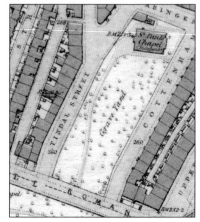

St Paul's from the 1860 OS map.

THE REDEWETTER MINSTREL: ROBERT ROXBY (1767–1846)

Orphaned as a child in the Redesdale area of Northumberland, Robert was brought up on a local farm. A life in agriculture failed to appeal and it was not long before he headed for Newcastle where the rest of his working life was spent as a bank clerk.

His rhythmical letters sent back to his friends in rural Northumberland proved popular and eventually began to appear in print. His later ballad poems were illustrated by Thomas Bewick. Always an enthusiastic angler, Robert and his friend, Thomas Doubleday (see page 153), began a series known as 'Fisher's Garlands' published annually for almost 25 years.

An' then farewell dear Coquet-side!
Aye gaily may thou rin,
An' lead thy waters sparkling on,
An' dash frae linn to linn;
Blithe be the music o' thy streams
An' banks through after-days,
An' blithe be every fisher's heart
Shall ever tread thy Braes

Roxby died at Westgate Hill and was interred in an unmarked grave at St Paul's churchyard in 1846. Fifty years later, a wall tablet paid for by public subscription was unveiled in St Nicholas' Cathedral (nave, north side) where Thomas Doubleday records:

'He was a warm friend, a trusty servant / An enlightened thinker and an honest man'.

St James' Parish Church

Benwell Lane

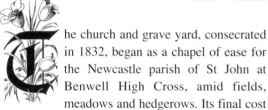

The church and grave yard, consecrated in 1832, began as a chapel of ease for the Newcastle parish of St John at Benwell High Cross, amid fields, meadows and hedgerows. Its final cost was relatively low at £1,668 because the land was donated by John Buddle, the mining engineer, and the building stone was gifted by John Hodgson, MP, of Elswick Hall. John Dobson designed the church, his first attempt at the Norman style.

St James became the parish church of Benwell in 1843. The building was extended as the population grew and in 1864 the original chapel became the chancel of the re-built church, which could now seat over 1000 people. In 1895 a spire with a clock and a peal of six bells was erected. A vestry was added on the south side of the church. In the late 1890s the original churchyard was extended by the acquisition of a large field on its west side.

Richard Grainger's railed tomb in front of the west side of St James' Church.

Who's Who in St James' Churchyard

Richard Grainger (1797-1861) Builder, developer, speculator

Richard Grainger was a local boy made good. The son of a quayside porter, he was born in a two-roomed upstairs tenement in High Friar Lane. One of five children, Richard luckily had three years of education, probably paid for by his industrious mother who earned extra cash by clear starching, glove making and sewing at home. He inherited her strong work ethic.

Leaving school at 12, he began an apprenticeship with a carpenter whom he later employed

as a foreman. Richard married Rachel Arundale, a Newcastle tanner's daughter (and Quaker) who was a good businesswoman. It is said that without her substantial dowry much of Newcastle's face-lift of the 1820s and 1830s would never have happened. During 19 years of marriage she gave birth to 13 children and some streets in the Elswick/Benwell area were named after them.

'While others *think*, Grainger *acts*' sums up Grainger's personality. He was a businessman of action and ambition, with an obsessive nature. Grainger's vision to replace large chunks of the old town with architectural gems in polished stone, was backed by some very able architects (including John Dobson), by the indomitable Town Clerk of Newcastle, John Clayton, who was able to smooth troubled

waters when necessary, and by a 2,000-strong dedicated work force. It is said that few townspeople at this time did not have at least one lodger, recruited from all over the country to work on this major project.

Blessed with early success, Richard bought Elswick Hall Estate plus 800 acres of surrounding land for development from John Hodgson MP and remarked 'I will stop at nothing until I have made Elswick Hall the

centre of Newcastle'. He also planned a botanical and zoological garden on the estate.

However after 1839 his Elswick ambition became drowned in a sea of debt and he found himself unable to repay loans and mortgages on time. He lived in Elswick Hall for only about two years before he fled to other parts of northern England to evade imprisonment for debt. It was only the ingenuity of John Clayton that allowed him to return to Newcastle, escape bankruptcy, and live the rest of his life with his children and servants at 5 Clayton Street West (now numbered 36 and marked with a wall plaque), in relative obscurity.

On the day of his funeral, bells tolled, shops closed for the day and thousands lined the route to Benwell churchyard. Memorials to him include a fountain in Waterloo Street, a wall tablet inside St John's Church (his parish church) and more recently a large metal plaque set into the road (now pedestrianised) at Grainger Street North inscribed: 'the past is my present to your future.'

JOHN BUDDLE (1773-1843) THE FIRST MINING ENGINEER

Buddle was born at Kyo near Tanfield, County Durham where his father had been first a miner and then the village's schoolmaster. Buddle senior was a gifted mathematician and was often asked to help at the local pit, making calculations, estimates and records.

The Buddle vault has no monument.

This led to his eventual employment as colliery manager at Greenside near Ryton. From here he moved to, and remained at, Wallsend where, after his death in 1806, his son followed him.

Under John Buddle's management, Wallsend became 'the most successful colliery in the kingdom'. He was a great innovator and several major improvements in mining techniques are credited to him. On the other hand, he was unconcerned about the use of children as cheap labour – mining should not 'dispense with the service of young boys'.

News of Buddle's reputation and achievements spread rapidly, and the Marquis of Londonerry, anxious to export his coal without being subject to monopolies on the Wear and Tyne, sought his help. He advised the Marquis to make a seaport town – Seaham Harbour – on his own estate at Seaham.

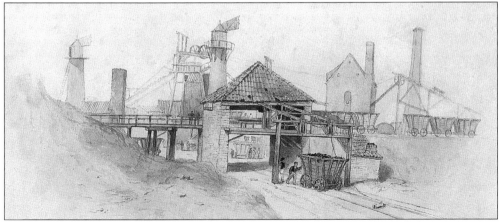

Hatton Gallery, University of Newcastle upon Tyne

Detail from T. Hair's watercolour of Church Pit Wallsend c.1838. Hair is buried in All Saints Cemetery.

Buddle was instrumental in the formation of the Mining Record Office, later incorporated into the North of England Mining Institute at Neville Hall, Westgate Road, Newcastle.

Buddle lies buried in a vault on land he donated. Designed by John Dobson, it is covered with large flagstones, without any monument or inscription above ground level. During the excavation to create the vault, a seam of coal was discovered, so the first ever mining engineer is interred within the material which was his life's work.

ARTHUR THOMAS LLOYD (1845-1907) THIRD BISHOP OF NEWCASTLE

Arthur T. Lloyd was well known to many Novocastrians before his installation as the third

Bishop of the Anglican Diocese of Newcastle in 1903. He had already been vicar of St Nicholas' Cathedral from 1882 to 1894, was an able speaker who could fill the Cathedral every Sunday evening, held no extreme views and appealed to most religious denominations.

Lloyd had previously turned down the Bishopric of Labuan because his medical advisor considered the tropical climate of Borneo unsuitable.

After only four years in office, Bishop Lloyd died at Benwell Towers. A fine recumbent alabaster effigy of him, complete with gothic tomb chest and canopy, by F.W. Pomeroy, is in the north aisle of the chancel of St Nicholas' Cathedral.

WILLIAM ISAAC COOKSON (1812-1888) INDUSTRIALIST

Cookson's great, great, grandfather, the son of a Penrith brazier, arrived on Tyneside early in the 18th century to seek his fortune and is recorded in 1721 as 'casting iron and brasswares' at Gateshead. Later the firm became involved in glass, salt and chemical production. Their boom period occurred during the Napoleonic Wars with large Government contracts for armaments.

As a 20 year old, William spent about a year working in Michael Faraday's laboratory, which must have been of enormous value in a scientific career that led to him patenting at least three important inventions. In the mid-19th century, William switched from glass to lead manufacture, greatly increasing the company's pros-

perity. He lived in Newcastle for many years at Eldon Square and Benwell Hall, before retiring at 53 to Yorkshire. He died at Worksop Manor in Nottinghamshire, leaving a fortune of £592,000. He was twice married (his first wife lies beside him in this vault) and left six daughters and five sons.

HENRY MILVAIN (1804-1890) RAGS TO RICHES SHIPOWNER

When he was 17 years old Henry Milvain borrowed £1 from his mother to travel from his Scottish home to search for employment in Newcastle. Following an apprenticeship to a draper and several successful years in that business, Henry turned his attention to shipping, becoming one of the largest ship owners on Tyneside and also a River Tyne Commissioner. Success in his life, he once remarked, was due as much to thrift – not to say meanness – as anything else. He sailed his ships uninsured, and was exceptionally lucky not to meet with disaster. He lived at North Elswick Hall for over 40 years. He proposed the building of a hospital on the site of the Workhouse at the top of Westgate Hill and later laid the foundation stone (uninscribed) of the buildings now known as Newcastle General Hospital. The Sacred Heart High School and Milvain Avenue now occupy the site of North Elswick Hall. An inscribed marble tablet is set in a stone pedimented arcade on the south (outside) wall of the church above a stone covering the entrance to his vault. There is also a stained glass window to his memory.

SIR WALTER SCOTT (1826-1910) BUILDING CONTRACTOR AND PUBLISHER

Born in Cumberland, and a successful teenage wrestler, Scott was a familiar figure in Victorian Newcastle. He started off as a mason on the new Central Station in 1848 and went on to own collieries, steel, iron and chemical works. He also built railways in Ireland and England and was contractor for London's first underground electric railway. This energetic man also owned the Mammoth Publishing Works in Felling and brought out popular editions of the classics. He had just enough time left over to be councillor for High Elswick 1881-1890. A generous benefactor of St James' Church, he died and is buried in France.

WESTGATE HILL GENERAL CEMETERY

WEST ROAD

By the 1820s little space remained for the burial of Newcastle's dead. The town's churchyards were at breaking point and at Ballast Hills (the only other public burial place in the vicinity of Newcastle) the area was 'emphatically crowded', inconvenient for travellers and suffering from 'nightly depravations of a horrific nature'.

A new cemetery was desperately needed. An exploratory meeting took place in 1824 at the Tuthill Stairs Chapel, but it was a further four years before the ideal location was found at Westgate Hill. The eventual triangular three acre site at the junction of the Carlisle Road and Elswick Lane was sold by John Hodgson Hinde, MP, of Elswick Hall, to the newly-formed Westgate Hill General Cemetery Company for £1,500, a sum said to be half the going rate for nearby building sites. The greater part of the site had been worked as a stone quarry.

This was intended to be a private cemetery, open to all religious groups, with all the advantages of permanency, secure gates and walls, adequate supervision, brick lined vaults and identifiable plots. More importantly the site was perfectly dry. There was a growing demand for dry burial grounds where loved ones were not transferred into 'pools of offensive water'. One of the first ten private cemeteries in England, it was never consecrated.

John Green and James Baker were appointed architects and work began shortly before the first interment on 18th October 1829, when 31 year old Mrs Elizabeth Angus was laid to rest ten feet down. Construction continued until 1831 and included high walls surmounted by iron railings, a house for the sexton with a chapel and register office (now demolished), serpentine paths and landscaping, modelled on Père

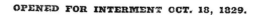

OPENED FOR INTERMENT OCT. 18, 1829.

ENTRANCE

The triangular plot was laid out in an ornamental manner between Carlisle Road and Elswick Lane.

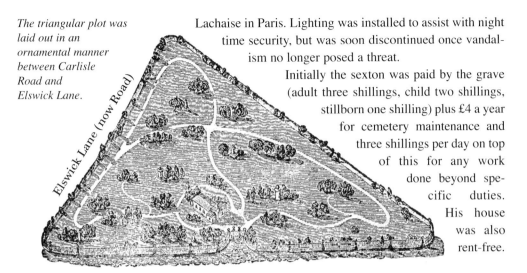

Carlisle Road (now West Road)

Lachaise in Paris. Lighting was installed to assist with night time security, but was soon discontinued once vandalism no longer posed a threat.

Initially the sexton was paid by the grave (adult three shillings, child two shillings, stillborn one shilling) plus £4 a year for cemetery maintenance and three shillings per day on top of this for any work done beyond specific duties. His house was also rent-free.

Westgate Hill Cemetery, 1900, looking west. Note the outward curving spiked railings to deter vandals. The 'Big Lamp' is in the foreground.

The sad remains of Westgate Hill Cemetery, looking towards Cottenham Street, in 2003. Some of the grave stones have been restored since this photograph was taken.

During the cholera outbreak of 1830-31 part of the cemetery was set aside for the burial of victims of the disease. Later a few trees were planted in a straight line to designate the burial area. Throughout the first 15 years there were around five burials per week, amounting to nearly 4000 in total. Later the paths were dug up to accommodate even more burials. The last burial took place around 1960.

In one corner of the cemetery there were at one time 1914-18 war headstones installed by the Imperial War Graves Commission – there is no sign of these memorials today.

WHO'S WHO IN WESTGATE HILL CEMETERY

CALEB ANGAS (1742-1831) COACH MAKER AND INDUSTRIALIST

Angas studied coach and carriage building in London before opening a similar business at the Bigg Market in 1780. He imported mahogany and other woods for the business direct from British Honduras in his own ships supervised by one of his seven sons. The business became the largest of its kind outside of London. Caleb's youngest son, George

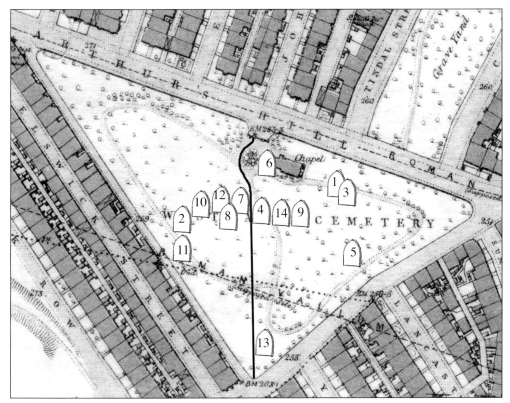

This map shows the current footpath with the cemetery layout as it was in 1860. The site of each grave is approximately at the centre of the base of the symbol. St Paul's graveyard is top right.

1. Caleb Angas
2. Henry Angus
3. Elizabeth Angus
4. The I'Anson memorial
5. John Bruce
6. William Davidson
7. Paddy Freeman
8. Robert Hood Haggie
9. Eneas Mackenzie

10. *John and Edward Richardson
11. John Fenwick
12. James Wilkie
13. Corsair, infant son of Native Americans
14. *Joshua Watson
* untraced gravestones, approximate position.
In unmarked graves are James Crozer and Jack Stephenson.

Fife, emigrated to Australia to become one of the fathers and founders of South Australia and was sufficiently well thought of to have a town, Angaston, named after him. Another son was drowned in the Bay of Honduras.

Caleb Angas also owned a copperas factory in the Lower Ouseburn area of Newcastle which produced sulphuric acid for the soap and glass industries.

HENRY ANGUS (1800-1872) COACH MAKER AND BAPTIST MAYOR

Henry was the son of a farmer, of Hindley in Northumberland, where Baptist services had been held since the 17th century. He was apprenticed to his relation Caleb Angas the coach maker (see above) and eventually took over the business. He was the first Baptist Mayor in Newcastle and worshipped at the Tuthill Stairs chapel. He stopped Sunday trading in the nearby Butcher Market and removed the hiring of servants from the Haymarket to the Corn Exchange. Henry married Hannah Sample, the daughter of a Baptist minister, who is also buried here.

ELIZABETH ANGUS 1798-1829 FIRST BURIAL IN WESTGATE HILL

Elizabeth was the wife of Joseph Angus of Forth Terrace. They were members of the well-known Angus/Angas family who worshipped at Tuthill Stairs Baptist chapel and were represented on the Cemetery Committee. Her funeral service was conducted with 'the greatest seriousness and propriety' by Baptist minister R. Pengilly on 18 October 1829 and the grave was dug ten feet deep 'and so well contrived that there was no apprehension of insecurity' (from grave robbers). The cemetery gates had not yet been hung, so security, at that time was still an issue.

THE I'ANSON FAMILY VAULT

This imposing monument (Grade II listed), now sadly in need of protection and repair, marks the burial vault of the I'Anson family. It was built by C. Burn and erected in 1873 for William Andrew I'Anson (1816-1872), a surgeon who lived just opposite the cemetery gates at Westgate Hill House (now demolished). He was noted for his kindness during the

Denton Hall c.1900.

cholera outbreaks. His son William Andrew (1848-1908), also a surgeon, was prosperous enough to live at Denton Hall, which he restored, from 1889.

JOHN BRUCE (1775-1834) HEADMASTER OF THE PERCY STREET ACADEMY

A magnificent monument to the memory of John Bruce, who died in 1834 aged 59, at one time overlooked the eastern end of Elswick Road. Designed by the well-known local architect, John Green, it consisted of a classical temple over a recumbent figure of Bruce. Bruce was founder and head of the eminent Percy Street Academy and father of Dr John Collingwood Bruce, antiquary and Roman Wall historian. One of his pupils was Robert Stephenson, joint designer with his father, George, of the *Rocket* railway engine. His

Above, all that remains of the once imposing monument that commemorated John Bruce. Left, the Percy Street Academy.

pupils and friends financed the memorial and it stood over a vault containing at least six other family members. Sadly the monument to John Bruce no longer exists.

WILLIAM DAVIDSON (1832-1854) VICTIM OF THE GREAT FIRE OF 1854

William Davidson was among those buried under collapsing masonry at Hillgate, Gateshead, during the Great Fire of 1854. He was the 22-year-old son of John Davidson, the owner of a substantial steam corn mill next door to the building which exploded and started the fire which killed 53, made 800 families homeless, and did £1 million of damage. William's signet ring was the only means of identifying him. Another casualty was Alexander Dobson, son of John Dobson the architect. He is buried in Jesmond Old Cemetery. William's father John then crossed the Tyne to establish the purpose-built Phoenix steam corn mill

Devastation on Newcastle Quayside after the fire of 6 October, 1854.

alongside the river at the Close – Dr Bruce described it as 'one of the marvels of modern times'. The double headstone records details of the Davidson and Revely families, related by marriage. Thomas Revely was Mayor of Gateshead 1846-7 and ran the Bluebell tavern in Bridge Street, Gateshead.

PADDY FREEMAN (1774-1840) FARMER AND MILLER

Originally from Windmill Hills, Gateshead, Freeman moved to High Heaton, Newcastle in the 1790s. Freeman's son worked at the mill in what is now Jesmond Dene. Later members of the Freeman family can be found in Jesmond Old Cemetery. The stone has been tipped over.

ROBERT HOOD HAGGIE (1810-1866) ROPE MANUFACTURER

The son of David Haggie, from Scotland, who began a rope works at Gateshead in about 1800, Robert Hood Haggie took over an existing ropery at Willington Quay (illustrated) in around 1840. It became the largest in England, employing more than 1,500 people. He lived in Summerhill Terrace in Newcastle and one of his daughters married Sir Arthur Munro Sutherland, shipowner. His grave stone is now fallen.

ENEAS MACKENZIE (1777-1832) PRINTER, PUBLISHER AND AUTHOR

Born in Aberdeen, Mackenzie moved to Newcastle when he was about three years old. His father wished him to become a shoemaker but Eneas was more interested in books and spent his pocket money on candles to read by.

He was one of the first to be baptised in the Tuthill Stairs Baptist Chapel – previous baptisms had taken place in the River Tyne at Paradise, near Scotswood. With John Moore Dent (also buried in this cemetery), Mackenzie set up Mackenzie & Dent, a printing and publishing business. A social reformer, radical and promoter of learning among the labouring classes, Mackenzie formed the Newcastle Mechanics Institute. He is best known for the magnificent volumes of his illustrated history of Northumberland and Newcastle, first published in 1811, copies of which can be seen in Newcastle's City Library. He died of cholera in 1832. His obelisk has toppled over.

JOHN (1799-1859) AND EDWARD (1805-1863) RICHARDSON, TANNERS

If you research the history of Newcastle and Gateshead the names of Quaker families such as the Richardsons, the Spence Watsons and the Peases crop up time and time again. They were energetic and generous Victorians who pushed forward local industry, establishing dynasties.

Originally the Richardsons were farmers in North Yorkshire and only diversified into the tanning of skins and hides to supplement their income after a poor harvest. It is said they had the concession to supply leather to Cromwell's army in the 17th century. The family reached Tyneside in the mid-18th century, but because of their Quaker beliefs found it difficult to set up in Newcastle so settled for a tannery at North Shields. Isaac, the father of John and Edward, moved the tannery from North Shields into Newcastle, just outside the Pilgrim Gate in 1784 and, six years later, to Newgate, now the site of the Co-op building.

Edward Richardson.

The brothers inherited the Newgate tannery and quickly began to mechanise. A windmill to grind the tan bark was followed by a steam beam engine. John and Edward were neighbours in Summerhill Grove and walked to work together most days.

Between them John and Edward had 23 gifted children,some of whom married men such as John Wigham Richardson, the shipbuilder; Robert Spence Watson of Bensham Grove; John T. Merz, the scientist and Thomas Pumphrey the coffee dealer. John Richardson's son David

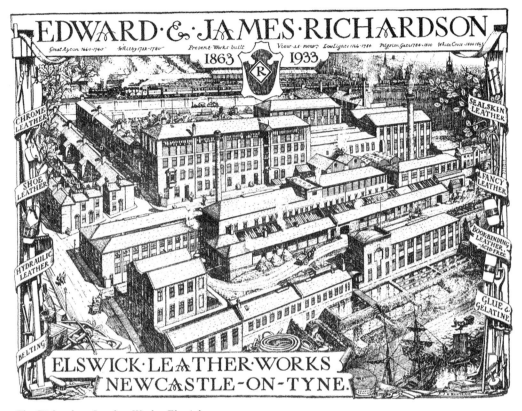

The Richardson Leather Works, Elswick.

married into the well known Fry family and John's great grandson was the actor Sir Ralph Richardson.

The collapse of the Northumberland and Durham District Bank in 1857, in which they were both major shareholders, affected both brothers seriously. John died of apoplexy two years later while holidaying in the Lake District. Edward, always in delicate health was forced to economise by moving to a smaller house. He died a few months after a major fire at the Newgate works in 1863. A purpose built tannery and leather works opened at Elswick the same year and survived there for over 100 years. Their separate family gravestones lie untraced, below ground level.

JOHN FENWICK (1787-1867) LAWYER

Fenwick's elaborate Gothic monument was designed by Benjamin Green. Born in Hexham, the son of a saddler, Fenwick was taught navigation and went to sea as a cabin boy, aged 14. He was promoted to the cook's galley but left the sea to study law. In 1814, he married Ann Rumney, the daughter of the headmaster of Alnwick Grammar School. Fenwick earned the nickname 'John the Baptist' because of his staunch and argumentative devotion to the Baptist faith. A friend, early legal adviser and business associate of Richard Grainger, Fenwick began the movement for a non-conformist cemetery in Newcastle and was an early member and treasurer of the Newcastle Society of Antiquaries.

JAMES CROZER (1813-1888) ALIAS DIRTY DICK, ECCENTRIC PHARMACIST

Born in Alnwick, Crozer was one of nine children of a nurseryman. He served a seven year apprenticeship as a chemist, but unable to settle down, he travelled the world for around 30 years as pharmacist, school teacher, labourer and ship's surgeon.

At the age of 54, he opened a pharmacy on Clayton Street. He slept on the floor in the back of the shop, lived on rice and tea, and wore a white cotton suit night and day, neglecting his personal appearance. Despite this, his business was very successful – people queued for a consultation and a personalised cure. Prices were adjusted to suit different types of customer and the genuine poor were never charged. A break-in convinced him to install wooden shutters which were never taken down – this made him even more mysterious and popular as well as making the shop easier to find.

At 72 Crozer retired to Brandling Village where his wealth was estimated at nearly £4,000 – mostly in a Chinese bank account. J.R. Forster succeeded Dirty Dick at the Clayton Street pharmacy and removed the shutters. The next shop occupant, A. Conroy, realised the value of Dirty Dick's reputation and philosophy, promptly restored the shutters and declared 'not to fit the case to a particular bottle, but to fit the bottle to a particular case'. Success followed. Though

there is no headstone – presumably there was nobody to erect one – Crozer's death notice in a local paper for 1888 notes that he was buried at Westgate Hill.

JOHN (JACK) STEPHENSON (1789-1831) ENGINEWRIGHT

In an unmarked grave lie the remains of Jack Stephenson, the youngest brother of George Stephenson, railway pioneer. At a time when factories had the bare minimum of equipment and most work was hands-on, Jack was working at the Robert Stephenson Works in South Street – the first purpose-built locomotive factory in the world. He died when a pair of sheer legs (for lifting) fell over, fracturing his skull. He was killed instantly, leaving a widow and four children. Nearly 200 friends and workmates attended the funeral. Two other members of the family also

Courtesy Jeremy Beecham

Robert Stephenson Works, South Street. Locomotives were built here from 1823 until 1901. Part of the works has now been restored by the Robert Stephenson Trust.

lie in the grave – brother-in-law Stephen Liddell who died as a result of another accident at South Street, and his 18 year old son, Stephenson Liddell. George Stephenson is said to have supported the widows and children thereafter.

JAMES WILKIE (1762-1834) SURGEON AND APOTHECARY OF THE NEWCASTLE DISPENSARY

Wilkie's memorial was erected by the Governors of the Dispensary as 'a mark of respect for his humane and faithful services over a period of 50 years'. The snake wrapped around the tree represents the Fall of Man and signifies Sin and Death. Wilkie's son succeeded his father as a resident surgeon and apothecary. In 1838, at the age of 40, he jumped to his death from a first floor window of a commercial lodging house in Grey Street. The coroner's verdict was temporary insanity. Despite a request for privacy, 1000 mourners attended his funeral. He, too, is buried in this grave.

CORSAIR, INFANT SON OF NATIVE AMERICANS

A troupe of American Indians from 'Ioway' (Iowa) arrived in Newcastle in 1845 'for the purpose of exhibiting their war dances and rehearsing the savage songs with which they celebrate their barbarian and bloody exploits'. The Ioway Indians spent nearly a week in Newcastle where they 'excited much attention' – Anna Richardson, a member of the famous Richardson Quaker family, felt it was unhealthy entertainment.

John Wigham Richardson (then about eight years old) wrote many years later: 'we youngsters dreamed of buffaloes and tomahawks, moccasins, bows and arrows and of the solemn forests and plains of the Great West. I shall never forget the delight of seeing them rub two pieces of wood together and then blowing up a fire.'

Newcastle Quakers visited the Indians and found: 'a party of 14 Indians squatting on the floor of

a small apartment, baby strapped in its cradle, and looking comfortable, having a crown of bells to jingle when it pleased – and White Cloud's little daughter running about amongst us'. The Indians appeared to have remained unconvinced by the Richardsons' attempt to reform them.

The young son of Walking Rain died in Dundee soon after their Newcastle visit. The family requested his burial in Newcastle, having enjoyed their stay there. Anna Richardson arranged this at Westgate Hill where some Quaker burials had already taken place.

The inscription on the ledger stone reads: 'The grave of Corsair infant son of Shon-ta-yiga and Okee-Weme North American Indians of the Ioway Tribe who died at Dundee 8th of 2nd month 1845 aged 8 months. The remains were interred at Newcastle by desire of the afflicted parents'.

JOSHUA WATSON (1771-1853) GRANDFATHER OF ROBERT SPENCE WATSON

Born near Allendale, Joshua became a cheesemonger in the Side where he lived over the shop. In the early 1800s he bought Bensham Grove as a country cottage and eventually lived there permanently. His son Joseph (1807-1874) married Sarah Spence, and became a solicitor and poet. Their son Robert Spence Watson (1837-1911), a solicitor, became very well-known and is buried in Jesmond Old Cemetery. He continued to live in the family home, Bensham Grove, which became a focus for social and political reformers and Quakers. The house is still there on Bensham Bank, and is marked by a plaque.

In 1849, at the age of 78, the energetic Joshua crossed the brand new High Level Bridge and its scaffolding, walking for part of the way on a single plank. His headstone was located near that of Eneas Mackenzie, but cannot now be traced.

Joshua Watson.

Bensham Grove, from a sketch.

CEMETERY AND CREMATORIUM

WEST ROAD

The cemetery and crematorium were opened in October 1934 at the cost of nearly £54,000. The architect was J.J. Hill. Contemporary comments stated that it was 'the only crematorium between Edinburgh and Darlington', it would 'solve Newcastle's burial problems for all time', and 'rank as one of the finest in Europe'. Features of the cemetery include

The loggia of the Crematorium in 1944 showing some of the memorial tablets fixed to the walls.

the 1939-45 War Memorial with around 40 headstones and the Snowdrop Remembrance Garden for children, stillborn babies and lost pregnancies, which opened in 1998. There is an area for Muslim burials in the South West section. Features of the crematorium, apart from the loggia, include a Garden of Remembrance for scattered ashes and a room containing a Book of Remembrance.

CREMATION: THE BACKGROUND

Cremation was popular in ancient times. Wandering peoples did not wish their corpses to be harmed by enemies, and incineration of the body prevented that. Greek soldiers killed on foreign battlefields would be cremated on the spot and their ashes brought home for a ceremonial

funeral – the greater the hero the higher the pyre. This custom was also followed by the Romans and many other European peoples. Following the adoption of Christianity in the west in the 4th century, burials became more popular. The Christian Church originally condemned cremation because of belief in the resurrection of the body on the Day of Judgement. In addition cremations usually required large pyres of wood, which threatened future timber supplies. Eventually the lack of burial space in churchyards forced a change of heart. The private cemeteries and large municipal cemeteries of the 19th century eased pressure for a while, but other methods were also considered by the government including perishable coffins and burial at sea.

Another idea was the London Pyramid, a multi-storey cemetery designed in 1824 for an 18-acre site in North London. Had it been built it would have become London's tallest building, its volume exceeding that of the Great Pyramid at Giza, Egypt, and able to accommodate over 5 million London citizens. However, its promoter failed to attract sufficient backers.

In 1873 Queen Victoria's physician, Sir Henry Thompson, visited the Vienna Exhibition and was impressed by a cremation chamber developed by Italian pioneers. His mind was made up and that year he published his recommendations on cremation and its advantages: cremation avoided the public health hazard of burial; the burial service could be conducted under cover; the fear of being buried alive that worried many Victorians would be allayed (two doctors were needed to approve a cremation); finally, the ashes could be used as fertiliser. During 1874 Thompson organised the Cremation Society of England, with others including novelist Anthony Trollope and painter Sir John Everett Millais.

Despite anti-cremation pressure from the Church and the courts (which were afraid that criminal evidence could be destroyed), land was acquired in Woking where Thompson developed a crematorium in 1879 in which a horse was reduced to ashes in under two hours.

However, cremation was still regarded as illegal until, in 1884, a Welsh Druid high priest cremated the body of his deceased infant son on a Welsh hillside. He was arrested but at his trial the judge decided that 'no nuisance had been caused to others' and that cremation was legal.

Early in 1885 the first official cremation took place in Britain, at Woking Crematorium, and other cities and towns followed. Queen Victoria, however, remained unconvinced and lies in the Royal Mausoleum at Frogmore, Windsor.

Until 1932 less that one per cent of deaths resulted in cremation. By 1991 that figure had risen to 71 per cent.

Today the Orthodox Jewish religion continues to forbid cremation; Roman Catholics accept it provided the funeral service is conducted first; and the UK ranks third in the world after India and Japan for the highest percentage of cremations.

St Mary's Roman Catholic Cathedral

Clayton Street West

After serving nearly 50 years as a Roman Catholic priest in Newcastle, James Worswick master-minded the idea of a larger church at Clayton Street West, which was to become St Mary's Roman Catholic Cathedral. By the late 1830s his 'back garden' brick church, behind his Pilgrim Street house, was proving too small and inconvenient for the increasing number of worshippers. In 1842 he acquired a triangular plot of land in Clayton Street West, partly on the site of the Forth recreation ground and opposite Richard Grainger's newly-built terraced houses. A.W.N. Pugin, the renowned architect who specialised in Gothic revival designs, planned the new building. Built in the 'decorated' style and reminiscent of 14th century architecture, it has pointed arches and windows containing geometric patterns.

The cramped nature of the site prevented a conventional east-west church and instead is, unusually, three gabled roofs wide to accommodate a large congregation (about 1,200).

It cost about £10,000 and the tower and steeple could not be afforded at the time of building. The church opened in 1844. Cathedral status was granted in 1850. In 1872 the tower and steeple were added, thanks to a legacy from the late Miss Elizabeth Dunn. The Dunn family had contributed generously to the initial building, including some stained glass windows – each one featuring the Dunn family crest.

Dunn & Hansom were the architects for the tower and steeple which, when completed, was the highest in town at 222ft Hansom, incidentally, belonged to the family that, in 1834, patented the Hansom Cab.

St Mary's Cathedral, Newcastle upon Tyne

Only two people (both former priests) are buried within the church, James Worswick, interred in 1843 'as the church grew around him', and John Lewis Eyre, an assistant to Worswick. Eyre was originally buried in 1842 at Jesmond Old Cemetery, exhumed two years later, and re-interred in a vault below the floor.

Outside the church only two burials have taken place. Bishop William Riddell and Rev.William Fletcher were both interred in the same vault and then covered by an elaborate chest tomb. Further burials both inside and outside the church were prevented by the Act of Parliament in the mid 1850s, forbidding urban interments.

In the Cathedral gardens, overlooking Neville Street, stands a bronze sculpture of the late Cardinal Basil Hume (1923-1999, see page 94). Queen Elizabeth unveiled the statue in 2002.

JAMES WORSWICK (1771-1843) CATHOLIC PRIEST

He died before the church's completion and lies buried in a vault in the nave. The brass cross once covering the vault was later moved to the Chapel of the Blessed Sacrament for preservation purposes.

A native of Lancaster and the sixth son of a wealthy banker, his training for the priest-

FATHER WORSWICK

Catholic Chapel, Carliol Sqr. 1833

hood in France was interrupted by the Revolution in 1789 and he only escaped back to England with assistance from the Duke of York and the allied armies. His studies continued at Crook Hall, until his appointment as priest to the secular mission operating in a dilapidated old house at Bell's Court (off Newgate Street) in Newcastle.

Following increased religious toleration, he acquired a house in Pilgrim Street and at its rear, in a long garden stretching down to the Erick Burn, a brick church measuring 85ft x 36ft was built as illustrated here. It is said that the first High Mass in Newcastle for about 250 years was said here.

Development of the Manors area in the 1870s involved the demolition of Worswick's back garden church and the construction nearby of the present church, also dedicated to St Andrew, which opened in 1875. The name Worswick Street preserves the memory of James Worswick.

William Riddell (1807-1847) Roman Catholic bishop

William, the third son of Ralph Riddell, a breeder and trainer of well known racehorses, was determined to become a Roman Catholic priest and so uphold his family's staunch beliefs. An ancestor had been involved in the 18th century Derwentwater Rebellion. After studying for a while in Rome he returned to Newcastle in 1832 as assistant to the Rev. James Worswick. William became a bishop in 1843, and in the  following year conducted the pontifical high mass at the opening of St. Mary's RC Church. Only four years later, during an epidemic of typhoid in 1847, he contracted the fatal disease while comforting the sick, and died at his home in Charlotte Square, aged 40.

The large vaulted chamber outside the church, in which he was buried, was built to contain 20 coffins, on shelves below ground. Following the subsequent interment of the Rev. William Fletcher (another typhoid victim), in 1848, the vault was never re-opened. During construction of the new cloister and courtyard in 2003 the opportunity was taken to locate the burial vault. When discovered, this vault contained shelves for 20 coffins, 18 of them unoccupied. The architectural archaeologists who reopened the vault were of the opinion that 'it could be used for burials in the future'. The decorative chest tomb memorial was possibly designed by A.W.N. Pugin and shows the Bishop's initials, his coat of arms and him attending a sick person.

Sacred Heart Convent, Fenham

The Society of the Sacred Heart was founded in France in 1800 and arrived in England 42 years later to continue their educational work. They came to Newcastle in 1904 and moved to Fenham Hall in 1906 to establish a school and college. After a fire in 1908 it became St Mary's Teacher Training College for Girls, closing in 1985 to become a students' hall of residence. Over 40 headstones in the cemetery mark the resting place of former staff of St Mary's College.

ST ANN'S CHURCH

CITY ROAD

Churches dedicated to St Ann were uncommon in England until the reign of Queen Anne (1704-1714) when some were named as a compliment to her. St Ann's in Newcastle is much older.

In 1344 Robert of Byker granted a small plot of land to a hermit for the building of a chapel to cater for the expanding population of Sandgate. The Chapel was dedicated to St Mary the Virgin and her mother St Ann.

By the 16th century the Chapel appears to have been known only as St Ann's, because there are references to 'Great St Ann's Close' and 'Little St Ann's Close' when Newcastle Corporation acquired this part of Byker for, among other purposes, the dumping of ballast. During one of the frequent years of plague in the late 16th century the inhabitants of Newcastle escaped to various places outside the town walls

The neo-classical St Ann's Church.

including 'the meadows round St Ann's Chapel' where in a period of six months 509 plague victims were buried. A few years later, in 1597, the plague was so serious the Assizes were cancelled, 'St Ann's Chapel was adopted as a place of refuge' and Newcastle Corporation Accounts record a payment of '8s 1d for drink and bread to St Ann's Chapel this week'.

Burials at St Ann's continued until in 1762 Aubone Surtees (Newcastle Mayor and father of Bessie Surtees) declared that the medieval chapel was 'too small and ruinous' and that Newcastle Council would pay for a larger and more elegant building. A few years later a new chapel was completed, in the then fashionable Georgian style using stones from the recently dismantled Town Wall along the Quayside. It was local architect William Newton's first substantial commission.

The new church was rectangular and open plan with large windows to allow the congregation both to see and hear the whole service, which was not always possible in medieval churches. It had seating for 600. Both chapel and churchyard were consecrated in 1768.

St Ann's amid the fields of Byker c.1770.

No further burials took place for nearly 60 years until 1828 when George Henderson, a 54-year-old merchant from nearby St Ann's Row, was the first person to be buried in the new churchyard.

In 1831, the first of three major cholera attacks hit Newcastle. Because the four town parish churchyards were quickly overcrowded, St Ann's was one of three 'other' burial grounds used during this epidemic. The other two were at Ballast Hills and Westgate Hill.

In 1843 St Ann's became a church in a new parish. The last burial occurred in 1869. Nearly 30 headstones remain.

George Henderson's grave.

WHO'S WHO IN ST ANN'S CHURCHYARD

JOSEPH CRAWHALL (1793-1853)
ROPEMAKER AND ARTIST

Joseph left his native Allendale for Newcastle aged 16 (probably with his elder brother Thomas) where he began a ropemaking apprenticeship at Newcastle's largest wooden shipyard at St Peter's. In 1812 he took over the existing St Ann's ropery, opposite St Ann's church, to form his own business. It covered a four acre

The vandalised Crawhall family monument.

site, at the top of a slope above the Quayside with an entrance on the New Road (later City Road). Business prospered and at the Great Exhibition of 1851 the company won a medal for 'the excellence of their productions'.

About this time the artistic Joseph designed a tall chimney for his factory in the form of a coil of rope. It was unique in the UK, as well as being a conspicuous regional landmark. Apparently the rope was twisted the wrong way and there is a local tradition that the builder, when he realised his mistake, committed suicide. Because of its dangerous condition the chimney was carefully dismantled in 1961, each stone being numbered to make re-erection possible at another site following City Centre redevelopment. This never happened.

Joseph Crawhall.

Joseph was a fine painter in oils and watercolours as well as a caricaturist, lithographer, etcher and wood engraver. Thomas Bewick, the renowned wood engraver, was a close friend. Joseph often made amusing drawings for friends and even his business account books contained many sketches. His artistic gift was passed on to his son, Joseph, and grandson, also Joseph. The family lived at West House, Low Walker before moving to St Ann's House on the New Road. The entrance from the ropery to the house was made from a whale's jawbone. In 1835 J.W. Carmichael, the well-known local painter, completed a fine watercolour from the garden of St Ann's house, looking towards Newcastle.

The ropery with its decorative chimney on City Road in 1926.

Later the house became the Ouseburn Police Station, then an engineering works before it was demolished in 1992. Nearby Crawhall Road is the only remaining family connection.

Joseph was Mayor of Newcastle in 1849 and also a magistrate. He died at Stagshaw House, near Corbridge, aged 59.

The Crawhall family monument (illustrated page 126) in St Ann's Churchyard was vandalised many years ago and awaits restoration.

THOMAS COULTHARD (1779-1829) BREWER

Thomas Coulthard, a brewer, died on 22 Nov 1829. He was renowned as the heaviest man in the district and his coffin was probably the largest ever seen in Newcastle. Measuring 6ft 7^1/$_2$ins, long, 3ft 5 ins at the shoulders and 2ft 4^1/$_2$ins deep, it took 100 square feet of oak to construct. Apparently this only took into account space needed for the body as it did not include an outer shell and lead coffin.

Mr Coulthard was interred (probably with some difficulty) in St Ann's burial ground, witnessed by

An extra wide load: Thomas Coulthard's coffin.

an immense crowd of people, on 24th November. The illustration from Sykes Records claims to be an accurate 1:12 scale drawing of the coffin. There is no surviving stone.

THOMAS TOWARD (1799-1845)

There is a moving memorial to the family of Thomas Toward. Five of his children are buried with Thomas and his wife, Rebecca. Four of the children died in infancy and the fifth, two years after her father, at just 16 years, a testimony to infant mortality in the 19th century.

BALLAST HILLS BURIAL GROUND

FORD STREET, OUSEBURN

In 1649 a local historian commented on the Ballast Hills, 'where women upon their heads carried ballist which was taken forth of small ships which came empty for coales; which place was the first ballist shoare out of towne.' He added that the Ballast Hills were used for 'drying of cloths'.

The Ballast Hills are at the east end of Glasshouse Bridge, close to the Ouseburn, and situated immediately above the three glasshouses (established in about 1619) 'where plaine glasse for windows are made, which serveth most parts of the Kingdom'. This open waste area was chosen as a burial ground by nonconformists (in particular Scottish Presbyterians and French Huguenot

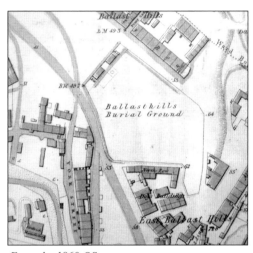

From the 1860 OS map.

immigrants) who did not want an established church funeral service in a parish churchyard. Ballast Hills also appealed to the poor of the established church, because the burial fee was only sixpence. There was no church. The site gradually shrank in size as new houses encroached and cinders spread from the nearby glassworks.

In 1785 local inhabitants complained about the disgraceful condition and mismanagement of the burial ground. It was reported that swine were 'rooting and grubbing' among the graves. Money was collected to build a wall to enclose the ground, plant trees and build a small house for the grave digger.

Ballast Hills became one of the largest nonconformist burial grounds in Britain outside of London. For many years there were at least 12 to 18 burials a week with more interments taking place here than in all the other Newcastle churchyards combined. Only a small proportion of graves were marked by stones (about 700 by 1827). The chalky, limy nature of the soil was said to 'accelerate decomposition', but by 1825 the cemetery was full. It was then enlarged to

just over three acres. In 1829 Westgate Hill burial ground was opened, serving all religious denominations.

The cemetery was closed in the 1850s and a public park created 40 years later with remaining stones used for footpaths.

Today many of the gravestones are very worn and cracked but a variety of occupations can still be made out, including blacksmith, bottlemaker, cabinet maker, cooper, joiner, keelman, linen draper, maltmaker, mason, master mariner, shipwright, silversmith, tallow chandler, tin plate worker, tobacconist, waterman and whitesmith.

Reproduced courtesy of Norman Burn

The author studies the stories told by the gravestones at Ballast Hills.

WHO'S WHO IN BALLAST HILLS

JAMES ROBERTSON (1758-1797) MINISTER OF THE SALLYPORT MEETING HOUSE

James was minister of the gospel in Sallyport meeting-house, Newcastle. His inscription reads:

> Modest, yet resolute in virtue's cause,
> Ambitious not of man's but God's applause;
> Swift was his race, with health and vigour blest,
> Soft was his passage to the land of rest;
> His work concluded e'er the day was done,
> Sudden the saviour stoop'd and caught him to
> his throne.

ROBERT GILCHRIST (1797-1844) SAILMAKER AND POET

Although there is no gravestone to Robert Gilchrist, a local poet and author, he was buried in the cemetery in 1844 aged 47. The son of a sailmaker, he took up his father's trade but was more interested in writing poetry and dialect songs, so the business declined. Gilchrist lived at

Shieldfield Green in the quaint 17th century house said to have been used by Charles I (while a prisoner in Newcastle in 1646/47) A plaque originally affixed to the building is preserved on a plinth next to the Green.

Also buried in Ballast Hills Cemetery is John Buchanan – one of the first Company of Missionaries sent out by the London Mission Society in 1796 – just one of many other ordinary men, women and children of Newcastle whose grave stones are now almost worn away. These were the wealthier occupants of Ballast Hills – most people were buried without a stone of any sort. Here is a small selection of the more legible stones.

C. Reid Silversmith of Newcastle, died 1794, may well be an ancestor of the well known Scottish family that founded several local businesses such as Reid's the Jewellers and Andrew Reid the Printers.

Andrew Bell, tallow chandler of Gateshead, was buried here in 1815. There was a huge trade in tallow candles (made from animal fats) because of their use in the mining industry. Soap was also derived from tallow and was a subsidiary industry to candle-making.

'Ralph Symington, Joiner and Elizabeth his Wife & Two of their Children Robert and Elizabeth died Young'. There is no other legible information on the stone.

The earliest date visible today relates to 'Thomas Davidson who died in March 1742 also Jane his wife and several of their cildren' [sic].

The oldest recorded stone (now disappeared) in the cemetery bore the date 1708.

William Robson Tinplate Worker and Sarah his Wife. Two of their Children died in infancy. Eleanor their Daughter died at Naples July 3rd 1806 aged 25 years.

Cuthbert Johnson was a tobacconist who died in 1839 aged 61. Three of his four children (also buried here) died before they reached the age of 21.

Thomas Nelson, Waterman, Catherine his Daughter died June 1848 aged 1 year

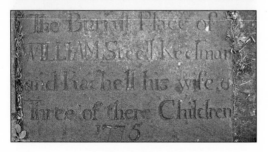

'William Steell Keelman and Rachell his wife & Three of there Children 1775' [sic].

BYKER AND HEATON CEMETERY

BENTON ROAD

As Byker and Heaton expanded in the 1880s, residents began to agitate for their own burial ground in east Newcastle. A major reason was that they were being charged double the normal burial fees to be interred at All Saints Cemetery on Jesmond Road. A 12 acre site near the Benton turnpike was secured. It was convenient because it linked, via Heaton Road, to all parts of Heaton and Byker and even better communications followed when Chillingham Road was completed. J.W. Taylor of Westgate Road was appointed architect and the cemetery opened on 24th April 1890.

In 1913 the size of the cemetery was doubled to about 24 acres. Two years later a section for Jewish interments was created within this extension.

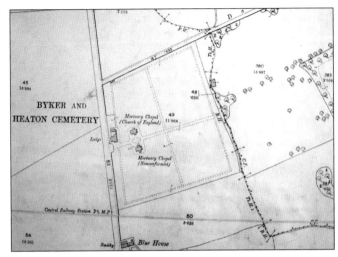

Malcolm Maybury

Top, the cemetery in 1895 in a rural High Heaton.
Below, the cemetery chapels in 1996.

WHO'S WHO IN BYKER AND HEATON CEMETERY

STEPHEN BROWNLOW (1828-1896) LANDSCAPE AND PORTRAIT PAINTER

Born in Newcastle, the son of a cordwainer, his talent for painting was obvious from an early age. Although taught by William Bell Scott, he did not become a full time professional artist until much later in life, starting his career as a boot maker at Byker Hill.

Eventually he opened a studio at 22 New Bridge Street, Newcastle near to his friend and fellow painter, Ralph Hedley. From 1878 he exhibited regularly in Newcastle. 'The Shrimp Girl', 'Sunset on the Tyne', 'The Poacher', 'The Busy Tyne' are some of his better known paintings.

Shipley Art Gallery

Ralph Hedley painted his friend, Stephen Brownlow, in his studio in 1892.

Ralph Hedley's painting 'My Neighbour' of 1892, shows Stephen Brownlow at work in his New Bridge Street studio. Ralph Hedley occupied this studio following the death of Brownlow.

CLAUDE A. COOPER (1931-1986) SHOWMAN

This former travelling showman had one of the most lavish funerals seen on Tyneside for many years. Apparently the staff of a local florist were preparing floral tributes until the early hours of the morning of the funeral and then needed three lorries and some hearses to transport them. They included a roundabout, a fruit machine, a boxing ring and a replica of the 'Tuxedo Princess' floating nightclub. Police were required to control traffic along the

route from St George's Church, Jesmond, to the cemetery because of the slow moving procession which included a horse-drawn glass sided hearse.

Claude Cooper bought the Spanish City at Whitley Bay, and as part of its revitalisation programme introduced the 'Corkscrew Ride'. He raised thousands of pounds for disabled and

handicapped children through the Variety Club of Great Britain.

His unusually large but low black tomb, over the family vault, required special permission from the City Council because it initially contravened cemetery regulations. It stands alongside a path close to other memorials of showmen.

LIONEL JACOBSON (1906-1978) CHAIRMAN OF JACKSON THE TAILORS

Lionel Jacobson, the son of a Russian immigrant escaping the pogroms, was born and spent his schooldays in Newcastle before taking a law degree at Oxford. He then practised as a barrister in London for a short while.

However, Lionel soon returned to Newcastle to join the family business, Jackson the Tailors. Eventually, as chairman of the group, he controlled some 600 retail shops employing about 6000 staff plus another 20,000 in its garment producing factories.

Known as Mr Lennie to all his employees, he always referred to them by their first name. He claimed: 'Anyone, even the office boy, can see me if the matter is important enough.' He also said: 'If you offer peanuts you can't expect to get anything but monkeys. Who wants monkeys to run a business?'

He always felt that a key factor in his success was his 15 minute daily walk with pen and paper ready to jot down new ideas.

Among his many donations to charity was the £120,000 to found a chair of clinical pharmacology at Newcastle University. He also contributed to a coronary unit at Newcastle's General Hospital.

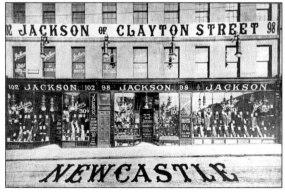

Lionel Jacobson in 1963, and below,
Jackson the Tailor, Clayton Street c1912.

PRIVATE EDWARD LAWSON V.C. (1873-1955) SOLDIER

Only two Newcastle soldiers have been awarded the Victoria Cross for outstanding bravery. One of these, Private Edward Lawson of the Gordon Highlanders, was part of the battalion that successfully stormed a heavily fortified hill at Dargai on India's North West frontier with Afghanistan in 1897. Aged 24 at the time, he rescued 2 soldiers under heavy fire from enemy tribesmen, despite being seriously wounded himself. Edward Lawson died locally aged 82. The Tyneside Joint Ex-Services Association met the cost of a new headstone erected in 1999.

ANGELO RISI (1860-1923) ICE CREAM MANUFACTURER

Perhaps the most striking monument in the cemetery lies alongside the main carriageway that divides the consecrated from the unconsecrated part of the cemetery. It covers the vault of the Risi family who emigrated from Italy in the 19th century, set up business as ice cream manufacturers in 1899, and are still actively involved in the catering trade.

Courtesy Risi family

The workforce in Wilfred Street c.1918. Angelo Risi is second left, his wife and son are far right.

CHRIST CHURCH

WALKER

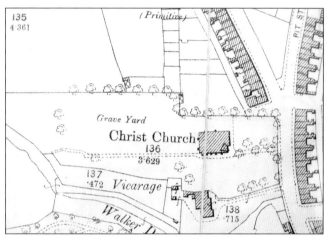

Before 1848 St Bartholomew's Church at Longbenton served as the parish church for Walker, even though it was situated four miles away. In fact, it was noted in 1825 that there was no school or meeting house of any kind in the area despite a population of several hundred. Walker had some of the earliest deep coalmines in North-East England and the ten pits in the area were at the forefront of pumping and ventilation technology. The nonconformists were the first religious groups to set up in Walker – the New Connection Methodists in 1838, Wesleyan Methodists in 1840, Presbyterians in 1846 and Welsh Independents in 1846 (there were Welsh ironworkers from the Port Talbot area living in Walker).

The Church of England first of all set up a congregation in the schoolroom of the Walker Iron and Alkali

Above, Christ Church, Walker, from the 1897 OS map.
Below, Christ Church in 1928.

Company in 1846. The foundation stone of the new church was laid in 1847 by the Mayor of Newcastle on land belonging to Newcastle Corporation. The architect was A.B. Higham (also the architect of Christ Church, Shieldfield) and the building was erected by contractor Richard Cail at a cost of £1,250. Christ Church was consecrated by the Bishop of Durham in 1848. It is a simple, solid building with a high pitched roof and the bell-gable at the west end. The tower and distinctive spire are at the east end of the nave. The east window was paid for by the Charles Mitchell Family.

The churchyard was originally 6,806 square yards but in 1864 three acres were added, and in 1899 a further seven acres. The 1899 enlargement was funded by John Wigham Richardson, the shipbuilder, and other large rate payers of Walker, partly because they did not approve of Urban Councils managing churchyards. They also appreciated the advantage of large open areas. In his will Richardson made provision for maintaining the churchyard 'in beauty and order'.

Christ Church became the largest parish churchyard (not cemetery) in Britain and featured in the Guinness Book of Records in the early 1970s. Burials today are only allowed where space is available in existing graves.

WHO'S WHO IN CHRIST CHURCH CHURCHYARD

ROBERT CHAMBERS (1831-1868)
WORLD CHAMPION OARSMAN

One of the most popular individuals ever to hail from Tyneside, 'Honest Bob' Chambers became a household name. When he died over 50,000 people lined the mile and a half funeral route from Pottery Bank to Walker. The bells of St Nicholas' tolled and flags flew at half mast. For a limited period the public were able to view the deceased in his coffin, watched over by his heart-broken young widow.

Robert Chambers was born at St Anthony's, one of 15 children, and began work at 11 in Hawks Iron Works, reaching the position of puddler. Rowing was

a popular sport on Tyneside and Robert was coached by his friend the veteran rower Harry Clasper. Though he was of slight build, Chambers became a very successful oarsman and probably the world's greatest natural sculler. His rowing career spanned 16 years, 1852-1868. He took part in 109 events, winning 89 of them. He was the first Tyne oarsman to win the World Championship and for six years held the championship of the Thames.

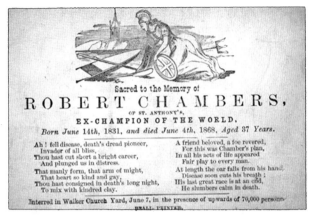

Robert Chambers' funeral card.

He died of TB at 37, in June 1868, at St Anthony's. Strenuous and incessant training would have made his illness worse. Harry Clasper was unable to attend the funeral because of illness, and he died two years later.

The memorial, funded by public subscription, was sculpted by George Burn from sandstone and erected in 1869. Now sadly headless, it shows Chambers dressed for rowing, resting on a river bank. The broken oar beside him has a masonic symbol on the blade, indicating that Robert may have been a mason or have been sponsored by them. Chamber's statue lies under a vaulted decorated Gothic style canopy. George Burn also sculpted another memorial to a rower, James Renforth, who died in 1871, which is outside the Shipley Art Gallery in Gateshead.

MONUMENT TO THE VICTIMS OF AN EXPLOSION AT WALKER COLLIERY, 1887

This monument was erected by the officials and workmen of Walker Colliery to the memory of eight men who lost their lives through an explosion at Walker Colliery (Ann Pit, Mitchell Street) in October 1887. It also commemorates John Dixon who lost his life in another accident at the pit on 2nd August 1887.

On 24th October 1887, 27 men were working underground when a deep mine explosion occurred at 1,200ft, about 540ft from the shaft bottom. There was little damage to the pit and few local residents were aware of the disaster but the blast was ferocious and all the bodies were charred beyond recognition.

Thankfully they were recovered within a few hours.

The Inquest Jury returned the following verdict: 'That John Pickard (and the other men) died in the Brockwell Seam of the pit at Low Walker Colliery … from burns received whilst at work, through an explosion in the westernmost north gate headway, resulting from a partially blown-out shot, fired for the purpose of removing stone, but as to who fired the shot there was not sufficient evidence to show; and that the explosion was due to coal dust, gas and air becoming ignited by the firing of the shot and was the result of pure accident'.

The victims are listed with their names and ages. It was a tragedy for the families of the men. John Pickard left nine children, most left widows, and it was Joseph Cockburn's first shift at the mine that day.

MONUMENT TO THE MEMORY OF THE WORKMEN KILLED IN A BOILER EXPLOSION AT WALKER IRON AND ALKALI WORKS, 1855

Coalmining led to the beginning of the Walker Alkali Company's works which is said to have been the birthplace of the Tyneside chemical trade. In 1797 John Losh, chemist, moved from Scotswood to Walker to take advantage of a salt spring that had halted coal extraction. His brother, William, managed the Works which became very successful. Salt for industrial purposes was not highly taxed, unlike domestic salt (a customs officer lived at the works to make sure the quality was industrial). They also used the salt to make soda used in the manufacture of glass and pottery. The works closed in 1891 following the discovery of huge salt deposits at Teesside, and the repeal of the salt tax.

William Losh founded the Walker Iron Works in 1809 next to the Alkali Works on the river front. This became Messrs Losh, Wilson and Bell as he was joined by Thomas Bell, manager and Thomas Wilson, accountant. Coal was cheap and plentiful, iron ore and limestone were imported as ballast, so the

Walker Iron Works c.1830s.

main ingredients for iron were on the spot. Losh, an engineer and inventor, worked with George Stephenson and Walker Iron Works became the largest foundry in the north of England, making the rails for the early railways, the castings for the High Level Bridge, and plates for shipbuilding. The Iron Works also closed in 1891 as cheap ballast imports came to an end and iron ore was found at Teesside. This monument is to eight men who died in a boiler explosion in the rolling mill on 8 October 1855. The two youngest victims were only ten years old.

THOMAS JAMES (1793-1858) BLAST FURNACE BUILDER AND MANAGER

A native of Merthyr Tydfil, Glamorganshire, Thomas died at Walker Iron Works on March 7th 1858 aged 65. The monument was erected by public subscription. There was a strong local connection with the iron works of Wales.

DANIEL JAMES OF WALKER (1796-1848) LATE OF DOWLAIS IRON WORKS

His stone states that he was manager at the Blast Furnaces Walker. Dowlais is a Welsh town near Merthyr Tydfil which in the early 19th century had the world's largest iron works with 5,000 employees.

WILLIAM SHORT (1811-1859) FOREMAN BOILER SMITH AT WALKER IRON WORKS

'Who died at sea January 17th 1859, aged 48 when on his passage to Smyrna for the benefit of his health'. Smyrna is on the Black Sea.

CONVENT OF THE GOOD SHEPHERD SISTERS BURIAL GROUND

BENTON PARK ROAD

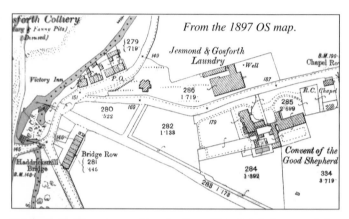

From the 1897 OS map.

The Convent of the Good Shepherd took over the villa and buildings known as Benton Grange, on what is now Benton Park Road, in 1888 and used part of its surrounding land as a private burial ground.

Benton Grange was probably built for Matthew Liddell, manager of the nearby Gosforth Colliery (owned by the Brandling family), around the time it opened in 1829 with its celebrated grand subterranean ball (see page 153). Immediately to the east of Benton Grange stood Gosforth Row and Benton Row which, in the 1891 census, contained a coal mining community of around 630 persons.

In the same census, the Convent was home to 34 females of which 25 were laundry workers. Virtually all these laundresses were single, under 30 and generally natives of the North of England or Scotland.

The Convent was demolished in the early 1980s and replaced by a residential estate appropriately known as 'The Cloisters'. The private burial ground was tidied up and headstones replaced by a single memorial stone representing the '48 Good Shepherd Sisters and their Chaplain' for whom this was their last resting place.

St Bartholomew's Parish Church

Station Road, Benton

A church existed here by, at the latest, 1130. In 1339 Philip de Somerville made a gift of the church and some land in the parish to Balliol College, Oxford, 'for the perpetual maintenance of six scholars and a chaplain'.

The medieval nave was rebuilt in 1790 by William Newton. He laid new foundations outside the walls of the old structure. He also included a square tower with a short spire above the belfry at the west end. The medieval chancel was

The church in 1842.

rebuilt in 1855 at the expense of Balliol College, Oxford, when mining subsidence from Heaton Colliery was causing problems. The church was restored again in 1874-75 by R. J. Johnson and again in 1888 by W. S. Hicks.

The original churchyard, of around two acres, was closed to burials in 1874 except where graves were free from water and could be opened without exposing a coffin. Burials in the church were forbidden. A civil cemetery was added in the same year and extended some years later. The churchyard is looked after by the Parish and the cemetery by the Council. The octagonal church hall dates from 1980.

Two of the old ledger stones, originally in the chancel floor, are now preserved behind the lectern. One of these is to a John Fenwick dated 1581 whilst the other stone is to John Killingworth,

The church as it is today.

vicar of St Bartholomew's for 15 years, and dated 1587.

A modern stained glass window by L. Evetts (to replace an earlier one given by Dr Thomas Addison (1795-1860) as a memorial to his parents) was re-dedicated in 1993. Dr Addison, born at Longbenton, was the first to identify the medical condition known as Addison's disease.

The stone coffin outside the south wall of the chancel was discovered in 1835. Stone coffins were rarely buried deep and this may have accounted for its disturbed contents and missing cover.

WHO'S WHO IN ST BARTHOLOMEW'S CHURCHYARD

CHARLES MITCHELL (1820-1895) SHIPBUILDER

Born in Aberdeen, the son of a cooper, Charles was educated at the local academy. He began an engineering apprenticeship at 14 and practised draughtsmanship for up to two hours before beginning his 12 hour working day at 6am. In his spare time he made wooden ship models.

He moved to Tyneside aged 21 and was employed by fellow Aberdonian shipbuilder John Coutts. He was involved in designing the *QED*, the small innovative steam/sailing vessel which used water as ballast. *QED* marked the transition from the wooden sailing vessel to the iron, propeller-driven steamer.

The coped grave cover in front of Mitchell's obelisk is the resting place of C.S. Swan (see page 147).

After eight years in London widening his experience of marine engineering, and some continental travel to hone his language skills, Charles returned to Tyneside to open his own shipyard at Low Walker in 1852.

During the next 30 years Mitchell's shipyard launched 450 vessels of which about 40 per cent were for export worldwide. Russia was an important market and for a few years staff were seconded to St Petersburg to speed up manufacture.

Charles married Anne Swan of West Farm, Walker at Walker Parish Church and, apart from some valuable social and business connections, he also gained three brothers-in-law interested in shipbuilding (C.S. Swan, H.F. Swan and Richard Cooke). Their only surviving child, Charles William Mitchell, became a professional artist and played little part in shipbuilding.

The steam yacht Cumbria, built at Mitchell's Low Walker shipyard in 1881 for the Earl of Lowther, lies in the Tyne.

In 1869 Charles moved home from Low Walker (adjacent to his shipyard) to West Jesmond House and renamed it Jesmond Towers. The building is now part of La Sagesse School.

Charles financed the construction of St George's Church (much to the relief of the Bishop of Newcastle) in 1887-88. There is a Mitchell Avenue near to the church and a Mitchell Street at Low Walker.

On the day of Charles's funeral, the very long cortège from St George's Church, where the service took place, was augmented by a special relief train from New Bridge Street to Benton, stopping at Jesmond and Gosforth, and then returning from Benton immediately after the interment.

The Low Walker shipyard finally closed in 1948 and is today covered by engineering workshops.

CHARLES WILLIAM MITCHELL (1855-1903) ARTIST

Born in Walker, the only surviving child of Charles Mitchell, shipbuilder, Charles William inherited his father's artistic ability and studied art in Paris. He lived in London and between 1876 and 1889, exhibited at the Royal Academy. His most successful painting, *Hypatia* is now in Newcastle's Laing Art Gallery.

Charles returned to Tyneside in the late 1880s to concentrate on his father's business interests. He added a large studio to the family home at Jesmond Towers and worked hard to promote the arts in the North East. He revamped the Academy of Arts building in Blackett Street as an exhibition centre, was president of the Arts and Crafts Guild (Durham College of Science) and was one of the founders of the Pen and Palette Club.

The grave is enclosed within secure iron railings.

Charles William was director of some local companies, such as Armstrong, Whitworth & Co. Ltd, Newcastle and Gateshead Gas Co. and Wallsend Slipway Shipyard.

His charitable donations included a part extension to Walker Hospital and re-roofing and enlarging the chancel at Christ Church, Walker. He also gave the land behind St George's

The gallery at Jesmond Towers, 1910. It is now part of La Sagesse School.

Church, Jesmond, to the St George's Cricket Club (now the Northumberland County Tennis Ground). Charles Mitchell senior had already given at least £33,000 towards the expansion and renovation of Aberdeen University. Charles junior gave nearly £20,000 to clear the outstanding debt incurred on new buildings there. The new Graduation Hall became known as the Mitchell Hall and the tower extension as the Mitchell Tower.

CHARLES SHERITON SWAN (1831-1879) SHIPBUILDER, FOUNDER OF C.S. SWAN HUNTER AND WIGHAM RICHARDSON

Born at West Farm, Walker, Charles was one of 11 children and the second surviving son of William Swan and Ann Sheriton. His father was secretary of the North Shields Railway Company.

Charles was apprenticed with Charles Mitchell & Co. at the Low Walker Yard. He worked in Russia as an engineer, becoming managing director of the Volga Steamboat Company. In 1865 he succeeded younger brother, Henry Frederick, as manager of the Mitchell's yard at St Petersburg which had been building warships for the Russian navy since 1862. In 1871 he returned to Tyneside to become managing director of Wallsend Slipway Company, and in 1874 was appointed manager at the failing Wallsend shipyard of Coulson and Cooke by Charles Mitchell, now Swan's brother-in-law, who had taken it over. Within a few years the firm of C.S. Swan had become a success.

Charles was killed in a tragic accident in 1879 while returning from a visit to Russia on a Channel steamer. He took too close an interest in the new type of paddle wheel, slipped and fell overboard. He was hit by the wheel and sustained fatal injuries. His wife, suffering from seasickness, was unaware of the tragedy.

In 1880 George B. Hunter (see page 95) was recruited from Sunderland to replace Charles at the shipyard. He went into partnership with Charles's widow to form C.S. Swan & Hunter. In 1903, when tenders were invited to build the *Mauretania*, Swan & Hunter combined with John Wigham Richardson to form Swan Hunter & Wigham Richardson, a company large enough to bid for the contract.

HENRY FREDERICK SWAN (1842-1908) SHIPBUILDER

The brother of Charles Sheriton Swan, Henry was also apprenticed, aged 16, at his brother-in-law's shipyard, Charles Mitchell and Co.

At the age of 20, he was seconded to St Petersburg to superintend the construction of iron

warships for the Russian Navy. Three years and
five battleships later the Tsar presented him
with a valuable diamond snuffbox.

Returning to England, he took control
over the Walker shipyard following the ill
health of Charles Mitchell, and immediately up-graded all the machinery. Steamers
of every description were built at Walker,
including icebreakers and train ferries, but
his outstanding contribution was the development of the oil tanker. He was a great
authority on oil carrying vessels, took out
many patents during their evolution and designed,
in 1886, the first oil tank steamer to carry bulk petro-

leum across the Atlantic. At his death nearly half the world's oil tankers had originated at the
Walker shipyard.

Apart from several directorships in leading local shipbuilding and engineering companies
he was also a member of various professional bodies: Naval Architects, Engineers and
Shipbuilders, Civil Engineers, Iron and Steel Institute and Mining/Mechanical Engineers.
For 27 years he commanded the 2nd Voluntary Brigade of Northumberland Fusiliers, eventual-
ly as Honorary Colonel. On his retirement in 1902 he was created a Companion of the Bath.
He gave generously to Walker Parish Church.

Henry F. Swan, far right in the top hat, at the launch of the oil tanker Silverlip, 29 November 1902.

THOMAS GREENFIELD (1810-1836) MINER

Poor Thomas Greenfield, whose stone is to the east of the church, was killed in an accident at nearby Killingworth Colliery on 31 August, 1836, aged 26. Mining was a dangerous job, though well-paid. His stone tells the story, which ends with a rhyme.

West Moor Pit, Killingworth.

'As he was descending Killingworth Colliery, the chain broke and he fell down the shaft, a depth of 180 fathoms. In respect of his character as a friend, a son, and a Christian his comrades have subscribed to erect this stone.'

> *Think nothing strange that happens unto all*
> *my lots today, tomorrow yours may fall*
> *the chain it broke I in a moment fell*
> *and had not time to bid my friends farewell.*

JOHN EDWARD MORRIS 1862-1890 VICTIM OF A RAILWAY ACCIDENT

'In memory of my dear husband
John Edward Morris
Late of Dudley colliery
Who was killed in the railway
collision near Taunton
11 November 1890
on his journey home from South Africa
after an absence of 2 years
aged 28 years.'

A very sad memorial to a young man.

St Nicholas' Parish Church

Church Road, South Gosforth

A church dedicated to St Nicholas, which may well have been of Saxon origin, certainly existed on this spot by 1170, perhaps the oldest church in the district. It was rebuilt in 1799 to the design of architect John Dodds, enlarged by John Dobson 20 years later, and an eastern extension built by Hicks and Charlewood in 1913. This church served a large area (stables were provided) and, because it was the only churchyard close to the Great North Road for several miles, it received more than its fair share of 'travellers' who had either died or been murdered on the highway.

St Nicholas' in 1906, before the extension to the east end was built.

In 1863 an explosion at Coxlodge Colliery killed 19 men and boys. It received very little public attention and most of the bodies were interred in unmarked graves. Five of the boys were under 13 years of age.

The original churchyard was extended in the 19th and early 20th centuries, bringing its total area up to about seven acres. The search for a new cemetery began in 1934, when no more land was available. In 1943 Gosforth UDC opened Hollywood Avenue cemetery, adjacent to the Garden Village development of the 1920s (see page 162). Since burial records began in 1699, to 1969 when the churchyard finally closed (except for cremated remains), 16,783 burials have been recorded of which about one third were children under 14 years of age.

The marriage register records the wedding, in 1805, of Mary Clarke and Edward Moulton Barrett. Their 40 year old semi-invalid daughter Elizabeth, a poet, eloped from her seclusion at Wimpole Street, London, to marry the well known poet Robert Browning.

Who's who in St Nicholas' Churchyard, South Gosforth

Charles John Brandling (1769-1826) MP, land owner, and coal magnate

A stone vault 'of considerable proportions' was constructed in the churchyard for the burial of Charles John Brandling in 1826. Four large pillars mark each corner of the vault. The surrounding railings were removed during World War II. Seven other family members were interred here between 1826 and 1853. The rest of the family moved to Somerset but the line is now extinct.

The Brandlings were originally merchant adventurers and came into prominence from the early 1500's as sheriffs,

There are no inscriptions on the vault except for the name BRANDLING etched on a metal plate.

Mayors or MPs. Usually they were buried in St Nicholas' Church, Newcastle.

Arranged marriages brought more land and business over the centuries and they owned several Tyneside collieries. In 1760 Charles Brandling (father of Charles John) decided to move from Felling, to Gosforth and engaged James Paine to design his new house, later known as Gosforth House. His six sons and seven daughters were all born there. By 1852 the wealthy family was bankrupt, possibly through over-investment in railways and mining, and Gosforth House was sold, together with over 2,000 acres of land in 1880. Two years later a racecourse

appeared with grandstand, club, hotel and stabling.

Charles John inherited the family estate in 1802. Initially he continued his political lifestyle as MP for Newcastle but soon realised the need to devote more time to his coal interests and eventually stood down from politics.

George Stephenson lived close by at West Moor and amused the Brandlings by inventing a lamp to burn under water to catch fish at night in Gosforth Lake. The disastrous explosion in 1812 at Brandling's Felling pit led to the development of the safety lamp simultaneously by Sir Humphrey Davy and George Stephenson. The origin of the word 'Geordie' is thought to derive from the preference of Tyneside miners for Stephenson's lamp.

The Brandling name is remembered in Brandling Park, the Brandling Arms Hotel in Gosforth, the Brandling Villa Hotel, South Gosforth, and Brandling Village in Jesmond near the Jesmond coal mines which he owned. He also owned Gosforth Colliery, near St Nicholas', which was opened in 1829.

An electioneering song of 1812 recalls Newcastle MPs Brandling and Ridley (see page 20):

Brandling for ever, and Ridley for aye
Brandling and Ridley carries the day:
Brandling forever, and Ridley for aye:
There's plenty of coals on our waggon way!

(Note, at this date only landowners could vote in elections.)

Brandling, with his brother (Robert William) and brother-in-law (Matthew Bell), contributed largely to the rebuilding of Gosforth Parish Church in 1799.

Following his death, his brother, the Reverend Ralph Henry Brandling, inherited what turned out to be a disintegrating and eventually bankrupt estate. He moved to the continent as an economy measure. The 'last of the long roll of Brandlings of Gosforth and Felling', he had officiated at all the interments in the family vault (except his own of course).

Coal wagons on the Brandling Junction Railway, Gateshead, early 1840s.

The 'Main Dike' stone, near the entrance on Church Road, is one of two stones marking the line of a geological fault.

Charles John Brandling started to sink the shaft for Gosforth Colliery in 1825 but it was too close to the '90 fathom dike', an east-west land slip running across south-east Northumberland. The average drop or slippage was 90 fathoms or 540 feet. Over the next four years, the shaft was continued down, at great cost, to reach the slipped coal seam. To celebrate the eventual success in 1829 a ball took place 1,100ft below ground level. From 9.30am, 300-400 guests were lowered in baskets. Each person hewed a piece of coal as a souvenir. They danced until 3pm on a flagged floor with lamps and candles for lighting. Coxlodge Brass Band provided the music and refreshments of cold punch, malt liquor and biscuits were served.

THOMAS DOUBLEDAY (1790-1870) POET, DRAMATIST, BIOGRAPHER, RADICAL POLITICIAN

Thomas succeeded to the family soap manufacturing business (Doubleday and Easterby) in the Close but was more interested in literature than soap boiling. The business collapsed through insolvency and Thomas was offered a job as Registrar of Births, Marriages and Deaths at St Andrew's, Newcastle, then as secretary of the Coal Trade. He had a large circle of literary and political friends, was an outspoken Whig and supporter of Earl Grey's Reform Bill of 1832. Never successful in business, he was a well-respected poet and thinker. He collaborated with Robert Roxby on the 'Fisher's Garlands' (see page 100).

ANTHONY EASTERBY (1757-1844) SOAP MAKER

Soap manufacturer (with Thomas Doubleday, senior) in the Close. Soap was produced as a by-product of the immense demand for pit candles (animal fats were the main ingredients of both tallow candles and soap).

The soap factory proved a constant source of irritation to its next door neighbours at the Mansion House. The smell of the soap-making process 'resembled the smell of a rotten egg, gas and onions'. Even the great Michael Faraday could not solve the problem. It is said visitors often left the Mayor's table on account of the smell, although some people argued that these curtailed dinners saved the Corporation a good deal of expense. John Brandling, the sheriff, often refused the offer of overnight accommodation at the Mansion House. The factory was eventually forced to move away.

THOMAS HEDLEY (1809-1890) SOAP MAKER

Son of a Northumbrian sheep farmer, he began work as a clerk at a Gateshead firm of grocers, tallow chandlers and wine merchants. In 1838 the business, now specialising in soap production, moved to the City Soap Works on what became City Road, Newcastle. Hedley's financial flair made him a partner, then proprietor, and the business flourished. It was taken over by U.S. soapmakers, Proctor and Gamble, in 1930. Hedley was Mayor of Newcastle in 1863 and had several other directorships, he was also a JP and played a leading part in setting up a large psychiatric hospital at Coxlodge.

Hedley's City Soap Works, 1894. It made about 50 kinds of soap, including 'genuine brown scouring, best and curd mottled, Newcastle blue mottled, Newcastle grey mottled, genuine super extra honey …'

JAMES LOSH (1763-1833) BARRISTER

Born in Cumbria, Losh studied chemistry and theology at Cambridge. He soon gave up theology in favour of the law because of his Unitarian views. He became a barrister at Drury Lane (off Mosley Street, Newcastle) and lived in Jesmond Grove (now demolished). He was vice president of the Literary and Philosophical Society of Newcastle and a life-sized statue (by J.G. Lough) stands on the library staircase. A supporter of civil and religious liberty and parliamentary reform, he was chief spokesman of the Whig party. He was Recorder of Newcastle and an Honorary Freeman of the town. His brothers were all industrialists: John (1756-1814) founded the Walker Alkali Company; George (1766-1846) was a chemical manufacturer; and William (1770-1861) founded the Walker Iron Works with Thomas Wilson & Thomas Bell. He was a great supporter of the newly patented steam engine and was on the Board of the Newcastle-Carlisle Railway along with his brother William.

JOB BULMAN (1746-1818) GOSFORTH AND COXLODGE LANDOWNER

Bulman returned to Tyneside after a prosperous medical career in India and bought land on both sides of what is now Gosforth High Street. To give Bulman status as a landowner comparable to the Brandlings (and their Brandling Village) the words 'Bulman Village' were cut into the front of a stone house on Gosforth High Street, next to the Brandling Arms Hotel. He built Coxlodge Hall in 1796 – The Drive, Gosforth, was originally the carriageway to the hall. Bulman's son, Job James, lost the family money and had to sell off the land for development. In 1877 Thomas Hedley, the soap manufacturer, was living there (see page 154) when the Hall was badly damaged by fire. It was rebuilt, but demolished in 1938 soon after this photograph was taken.

THOMAS (1783-1856) AND WILLIAM SMITH (1787-1860) SHIPBUILDERS

The father of these brothers, Thomas Smith of Amble, took over Newcastle's largest wooden shipbuilding yard at St Peters in 1810. Thomas and William continued the business, specialising in the construction of many high class East India Ships. The 980 ton *Bucephalus*, then the largest

William Smith.

vessel built on the Tyne, was launched in 1840. By 1848, they needed extra space which they leased at North Shields. In 1871 St Peter's shipyard was sold to R. & W. Hawthorn and Smith's business moved to North Shields. Smith's Dock Company Ltd was formed in 1899 eventually becoming the world's largest ship-repairing business.

Smiths' shipyard at St Peter's c.1830.

WILLIAM BOYD BELL (1875-1886) CHOIRBOY

The burial of this 11 year old from Gosforth Colliery was thought to be 'the best attended and best reported in the Press of any in the Churchyard'. He suddenly took ill while playing with his friends. Sadly, doctors could do nothing and he died several hours later. Members of the congregation and the newly formed choir erected the monument.

JOHN DEES (1796-1849) MASON

Dees was killed by an explosion of gas at Gosforth Colliery on 14 June 1849. He was 53 years old. Thomas Forster aged 54 and John Lawson aged 32 were killed at the same time. It was the first fatal explosion at the colliery in 20 years. Gosforth, St Nicholas's church, and the Brandlings are all closely connected with Gosforth Colliery. The watercolour below, by Thomas Hair (buried in All Saints Cemetery, Jesmond) shows the pit around 1840. The waggonway took the coals down to the Tyne.

Gosforth Colliery

JOHN RAMSAY (1707-1782) AGED 75

Ye politicians stop and pause!
A patriot lieth here,
Who loved his country and its laws,
And liberty held dear.
To mathematicks he inclined,
His mind was always gay
An husband good, and parent kind,
Was Honest John Ramsay.

All we know about John Ramsay is in his epitaph.

ASHBURTON ROMAN CATHOLIC CEMETERY

GOSFORTH

An act of Parliament in 1866 allowed religious bodies to open industrial schools for children aged under 14. The aim was to protect vulnerable children and reduce juvenile crime. In Newcastle the Bishop Chadwick Memorial Industrial School for Boys had opened in 1882 in the old grandstand building belonging to the Town Moor racecourse. The Roman Catholic church was looking for suitable premises for a similar school for girls. In 1883 the owner of Ashburton Villa, one of very few houses in the area, sold his property, plus 14 acres of open land for £9,000. The villa became St Elizabeth's Industrial School for Girls and part of the land became the site for the Catholic Cemetery of the Holy Sepulchre. The cemetery opened in 1884 and at that time there were no surrounding residential developments. It is a small burial ground of about two acres approached from the south end of Wolsingham Road.

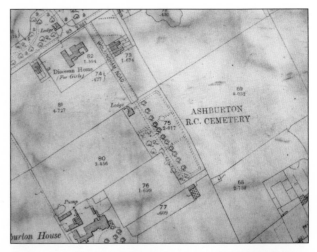

Above, from the 1897 OS map, and below, in 2003.

WHO'S WHO IN ASHBURTON CEMETERY

RT. REV. JOHN WILLIAM BEWICK (1824-1886) BISHOP AND FOUNDER OF ST CUTHBERT'S RC GRAMMAR SCHOOL

Born at Minsteracres in Northumberland, the home of the ancient Catholic Silvertop family, Rev. Bewick trained for the priesthood at Ushaw College. Ordained in 1850, he caught cholera, but recovered, while helping the sick and dying during the epidemic of 1853.

He became third Bishop of Hexham and Newcastle in 1882. As well as establishing the Industrial Schools in Gosforth for destitute boys and girls, he also helped found St Cuthbert's RC Grammar School, Bath Lane, which later moved to Benwell.

JOHN FARNON (1851-1923) DEPARTMENT STORE OWNER

An Irish linen importer, born in County Down Northern Ireland, he founded Farnon's Department Store in Nun Street (now Wilkinson's) in 1882, living above the shop for some time, with his wife Annie (née Richardson).

He was a councillor for Gosforth UDC for 25 years and chairman in 1917-18. He also served on the Newcastle School Board and as a JP for Newcastle. He donated the apse window to St Charles RC Church in Gosforth. His two surviving daughters donated the Lady Altar at St Charles Church in memory of their parents.

Try Farnons First, 1949.

NORTH GOSFORTH CEMETERY

NORTH GOSFORTH

Opened in 1878, North Gosforth is the smallest cemetery maintained by Newcastle City Council, with just over 4,000 interments to Oct 2002. About four miles north of the city centre, it mainly serves the Wideopen, Seaton Burn, Dudley, Dinnington, Hazelrigg areas.

The once large concentration of collieries in the area meant that there are numerous victims of mining accidents buried in the cemetery.

The gates to North Gosforth cemetery.

1881: Joseph Gascoigne – 'killed by a boiler explosion at Seaton Burn Colliery' aged 31.

1893: Robert Atchison – 'accidentally killed in the mine at Seaton Burn Colliery' aged 43 (illustrated).

Death did to me short warning give,
Therefore be careful how you live,
My weeping friends left behind,
I had not time to speak my mind.

1930: John Shield – 'died of injuries received at Dudley Colliery' aged 54.

NORTH GOSFORTH CHAPEL

MELTON PARK, GOSFORTH

Tucked away in the centre of the Melton Park residential estate in North Gosforth are the ruins of a small medieval chapel. It first appears in the records in 1256 when a thief sought sanctuary there. However, apart from its name St Nicholas' (because of its attachment to the mother church of St Nicholas' at Newcastle), little is known of its history.

Originally there was a small village, North Gosforth, in this area. By the late 18th century it was described as 'a small village in a low ground with a ruinous chapel'. No trace of this village remains today.

The chapel was probably burned down in the 17th century, but its attached burial ground is thought to have continued in use. In the 1780s a clergyman is known to have read a burial service there. Several tombstones and medieval grave slabs lie scattered around the ruins, embedded in the grass. The most easily read stone relates to a yeoman, William Hedley (died 1664), his wife and 12 children who lie buried here (illustrated). Their

epitaph follows:

> *In Christian hope one Rests Here*
> *Obscure yet Tender Shed a Teare*
> *He was a Godly Zealous youth*
> *Never deserting from the Truth*
> *Humilitie Love Honestie*
> *Each Vertue of Humanitie*
> *Did in him Florish while Here He*
> *Lived in Faith Hope and Charitie*
> *Ending this Life in Godly Sort*
> *Yielding to the World a good Report.*

His arms and crest appear below the epitaph. A less readable stone to John Robinson, also with armorial bearings, is adjacent.

HOLLYWOOD AVENUE CEMETERY

GARDEN VILLAGE, GOSFORTH

Hollywood Avenue cemetery was opened in 1943 by Gosforth U.D.C. because of lack of space in St Nicholas' Churchyard, Gosforth. It occupies what had been an open field to the east of the County Athletic Ground (now Asda supermarket). There have been around 4,050 interments to date. The Garden Village was developed in 1926 as a model village with its own bowling green and tennis courts, initially for railway employees who worked at the electric train repair sheds nearby.

VANISHED BURIAL GROUNDS

THE FORTH INFIRMARY BURIAL GROUND

ewcastle had no infirmary before 1751 but the onset of industrialisation highlighted the need for some sort of accident and emergency facilities. Following the lead given by other provincial towns, Newcastle opened its subscription lists to raise the necessary finance for a purpose-built infirmary. Meanwhile, temporary accommodation was opened in a substantial house in Gallowgate with space for 23 beds and rooms for medical facilities. This house had a long garden at the rear, stretching away to the Leazes, but it is not known whether any burial ground was attached.

After two and a half years at Gallowgate, the infirmary moved in 1753 to a site about where the Centre for Life is today, adjoining the area known as the Forth, where it was to remain for over 150 years. Eventually, pollution from surrounding industry and the railways, plus the need for more up-to-date premises, forced a move to a more suitable location at the edge of the Town

The Infirmary, the Forth, c.1855, from the south west.

Moor, not too far away from the Gallowgate area, where it all began. The Royal Victoria Infirmary opened in 1906.

The Forth infirmary had its own consecrated ground. In 1996 an archaeological excavation, using full protective clothing, took place before the construction of the International Centre for Life. The cemetery was small in area, surrounded by a high brick wall (about 3ft thick) with one entrance and a gridded system of burial plots. No headstones or coffin plates were recovered and it is thought wooden grave markers had identified the burial mounds.

Exhumations lasted a few months and eventually some 210 complete skeletons and around 400 dis-articulated skeletons were recovered. After use for about 90 years the burial ground closed in 1845 and several years later an extension wing to the infirmary (by John Dobson) covered the cemetery. In doing so several interments were disturbed and damaged. Evidence also suggests surgeons were experimenting for teaching purposes because many skeletons showed signs of dissection, amputation, cransectomy and trepanning and in one instance a coffin contained a stone slab to compensate for missing lower limbs. Three coffins were recovered intact, preserved by a particularly wet section of the cemetery, which revealed the use of recycled thin timber planks of Baltic pine for the coffins and though the bodies had decomposed, pieces of hair and finger nails remained. Wood shavings had been packed around the corpses.

It seemed usual to bury the deceased in their clothing (most of these burials related to persons with no next of kin to claim belongings) together with personal items such as cuff links, buttons and parts of footwear. Although many burials related to the local unclaimed poor, such as the pit boy with a fractured skull or the person run over by a wagon, burial registers later on confirmed a large increase in foreigners, perhaps seamen.

Because this exhumation would provide a unique opportunity to study the poorer section of society, the remains were sent to Sheffield for examination. Many medical conditions were diagnosed indicating tuberculosis, syphilis, rickets, bone cancer and dwarfism. Finally human remains were then separately boxed and interred at Lemington cemetery in 1998 where a sufficiently large burial area remained available.

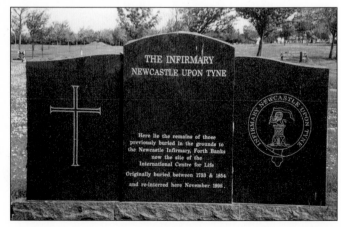

THE QUAKER BURIAL GROUND, PILGRIM STREET

For over 150 years the Society of Friends (Quakers) buried some of their dead behind their Meeting House in Pilgrim Street and for 40 years before that, at a site in Pipewellgate, Gateshead. The Quakers first reached Tyneside in 1657 but were repeatedly refused permission to settle in Newcastle because of opposition from the Church of England and so 'a little meeting was got up at the Gatesyde' across the Tyne where they had to endure continual persecution. The Toleration Act of 1689 relaxed some of the rules concerning non-conformity and several years later the Quakers were allowed to purchase a site in Pilgrim Street, Newcastle, for £120. They set up a Meeting House with burial ground, in what was then 'a rural locality of a main thoroughfare'. The building was completed about 1698.

The site had a narrow frontage on to Pilgrim Street, but stretched out about 100 yards at the rear down to the Erick Burn, a tributary of the Pandon Burn. Buildings mushroomed over the next two centuries and at one point the main Meeting Room could seat 552 persons. The burial ground lay behind these buildings. At least 440 interments took place here 1698-1850s. Many more occurred in nameless graves at the Ballast Hills Cemetery, Ouseburn, or in the gardens, fields and orchards of relations of the deceased. Generally, Quakers and other Non-Conformists did not wish to be buried in their parish churchyard because before 1880 only clergy of the established church could conduct the burial service, with no allowance for other rites.

 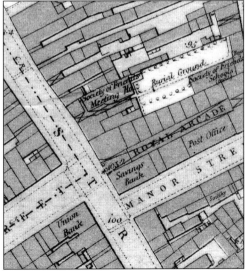

The door of the Friends Meeting House c.1890 and the 1860 OS map showing the Pilgrim Street site.

At first few Quakers had a headstone. They had long objected to the 'flattering inscriptions on gravestones' and in 1717 drew attention to the 'vain and empty custom of erecting monuments' over the dead and advised their removal 'with discretion and conveniency'. This attitude was relaxed in 1825 but there was still little enthusiasm for headstones at Pilgrim Street, probably because children from the nearby Quaker School used the cemetery as their play area. Deborah Richardson, grandmother of John Wigham Richardson (and great great grandmother of Sir Ralph Richardson) was one of those buried here (see page 114).

In 1961 the area was required for urban re-development and the Society of Friends eventually moved to premises at Jesmond Road. Today their Pilgrim Street site lies beneath the northern approaches of the roundabout. When they moved to Jesmond Road they took with them their large front door, the inscribed doorway keystone, and the Meeting Room benches. Bodies were exhumed from the cemetery and re-interred elsewhere at a rural meeting house.

Built into the garden wall at Jesmond Road Meeting House is a 'memorial' stone (illustrated) recording the death of Abigail Tizacke who died in 1679 aged only seven weeks. Her parents were Newcastle Quakers who had married at the Gateshead Meeting House. Her death was registered at Gateshead, where it is thought she would have been buried. The Tizackes were French Protestant glass workers who immigrated during the 17th century and this memorial stone was probably first laid in the garden of her parents home adjacent to the Ouseburn Glassworks.

UNITARIAN CHAPEL AND BURIAL GROUND, HANOVER SQUARE

The Unitarian Chapel in Hanover Square, which opened in 1727, had a small burial ground attached. Sources in the early 19th century stated 'it is very seldom used' and another added, 'none have been interred here except a child and Mr W. Robson and his wife'. William Robson had been a ship and keel builder on the North Shore and had contributed greatly to the establishment of the Royal Jubilee Schools (demolished) in 1810 on what is now City Road. This purpose-built chapel (illustrated) superseded a meeting house outside the Close Gate and was erected on vacant land originally held by the Carmelite or

White Friars. Already people were moving away from the congested Quayside and the plan was to surround the chapel with houses in the form of a square with fine views over the river and to name it after the then Royal family. In fact this speculative scheme never fully materialised. When opened the chapel could hold 600 people and early in its life, housed a charity school where 15 boys would be educated, clothed and placed with 'proper masters', all supported by voluntary subscriptions. In 1782 the Rev William Turner was appointed its pastor and he remained in post for 59 years until in 1841, aged 79, he retired to Manchester where he died at 97. An enthusiastic lecturer and schoolmaster, Turner was instrumental in founding the Newcastle Literary & Philosophical Society in 1793 at Low Friar Street. Several years earlier, in 1784, he had established at the Chapel, Newcastle's first Sunday School for boys and girls – second only in the UK to Robert Raike's Sunday School in Gloucester.

In 1854 the Unitarians moved to a larger purpose-built building in New Bridge Street and a tobacco/snuff factory eventually replaced the Hanover Square Chapel. The present Church of Divine Unity in Ellison Place dates from around 1940.

HOSPITAL OF ST MARY THE VIRGIN, WESTGATE

The 12th century Hospital of St Mary the Virgin stood on the present site of George Stephenson's monument at the junction of Westgate Road and Neville St. At that time the word 'hospital' had more to do with hospitality than medicine, the main purpose of the resident clergy being 'to serve God and the poor and to make it a place of entertainment for the indigent clergy and such pilgrims as were passing'. It was near to St Bartholomew's Nunnery whose sisters probably assisted with certain tasks, such as nursing, so saving the expense of hired staff. There was generous and continuous financial support by way of gifts, burial fees and legacies and at one time the hospital owned a large part of Newcastle in addition to 17 villages outside the town. Those who gave support usually expected prayers to be said for them and their families forever.

The Hospital consisted of a

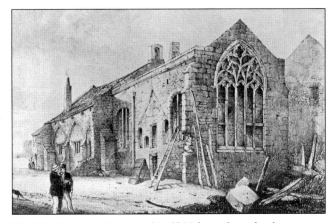

The Hospital chapel, removed in 1844 for railway development.

spacious room where men and women slept on opposite sides and where the luxury of one bed per person was anything but the norm. A large garden and orchard extended south to the river and the Forth before the building of the town wall in the 13th century. There was a chapel where the sick might worship their God with a permanent priest, and a graveyard. Evidence is scarce for burials but they would have taken place in the chancel of the chapel or in the graveyard, and in both cases fees would have been charged. In the 19th century, six grave covers and a stone coffin dating from the 12th to 15th centuries were recovered from the area.

The Hospital escaped damage at the Reformation, probably because it was more charitable than religious, and the Chapel became the home of the Grammar School for nearly 240 years before the buildings were swept away in 1844 to make way for Neville Street and other railway developments. All that remains is a gate pillar opposite Stephenson's monument and, in the grounds of the Royal Grammar School in Jesmond, two columns rescued from the Chapel.

THE ANGLO-SAXON CEMETERY AT CASTLE GARTH

Skeletons being excavated from the Anglo-Saxon cemetery at Castle Garth, 1990.

An extensive Anglo-Saxon cemetery has been investigated by archaeologists beneath and to the south of the railway arches at the Castle Keep, on the site of the Roman fort of Pons Aelius. The burials appear to have continued after the building of the first earthwork castle in 1080 (which was to give Newcastle its name). When the castle was rebuilt in stone some 90 years later, the graveyard was submerged. Archaeology has yielded a few hundred skeletons, men women and children, all facing east. Since no grave goods were recovered the burials are assumed to be Christian. There may have been a pre-Conquest church, probably of wood, nearby.

THE QUIGS BURYING GROUND IN SIDGATT

The 'Quigs Burying Plas in Sidgatt' was used by the more affluent Protestant non-conformists as their burial ground from 1683 to 1790. The term Quigs and Quicks is a corruption of 'Whigs' and is derived from some entries of burials found in the register of St Andrew's Church. The cemetery was situated on the east side of what is now St Thomas' Street, near its junction with Percy Street (formerly known as Sidgate). William Durant was forced to resign as a minister of the Established Church in 1662 because he objected to the introduction of the revised Book of Common Prayer. He was excommunicated and became a Congregational preacher. When he died in 1681, burial in consecrated ground was out of the question, and so he was interred in his garden, behind his home at the top of Pilgrim Street. One of his sons erected a memorial (in Latin) to mark his grave, which is now on display inside the Church of the Divine Unity in Ellison Place.

Durant's widow Jane is thought to have purchased the Percy Street site as a nonconformist burial ground. The first interment in this new cemetery is believed to have been her son, Dr John Durant, a physician who died in 1683. Jane most probably was also buried here along with the rest of her numerous family.

In 1765 Rev George Ogilvie of Silver Street was laid to rest here. If on a Sunday any of his congregation were drowsy he would order the 'Snuff Mill to be c'ad roond the east or west galleries'.

From 1786 the burial ground was gradually developed for new buildings including Bruce's academy. Forty years later several headstones remained and ex-school

The tall building to the rear is Bruce's Academy (see also page 111).

boys could remember using them as 'targets for stone throwing' as well as 'scampering over the graves of their grandfathers'. None of these memorial stones are known to have survived. Before the cemetery was finally redeveloped, over 50 skeletons were revealed; one was enclosed in a case of lime, maybe the victim of some malignant fever. All the bones were re-interred on site.

BARRAS BRIDGE BURIAL GROUND

The name Barras is believed to have originated as barrows (earthen grave mounds or tumuli) which by dialect changes over the centuries has emerged as Barras.

The Hospital of St Mary Magdalene, founded in the 12th century for lepers, stood just to the south of the bridge over the Pandon Burn (now Barras Bridge) but, for obvious reasons, well away from the medieval town. St Mary's Place stands on the site today. It is thought that the deceased from this hospital were buried in the open ground between the hospital and the bridge. The area became known as Maudlin Meadows. Today this area is partially covered by the Church of St Thomas the Martyr.

As leprosy became less of a killer, poor people who died of plague or pestilence were buried in Sick Man's Close which stretched across the Barras Bridge towards St James Chapel. During the demolition of St James Chapel in the 1790s to build houses, vast quantities of human bones were discovered.

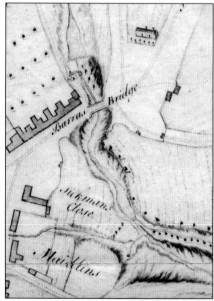

The site of the St Mary Magdalene Hospital (lower left) and Sickmans Close, from a 1746 map.

Remains of the Mary Magdalene Hospital, c.1820.

NUNS AND FRIARS

THE NUNNERY OF ST BARTHOLOMEW

This Benedictine nunnery, the first known monastic house in Newcastle, is mentioned in 1086 when the mother-in-law of King Malcolm of Scotland retired there. It was located on the site of the Grainger Market, but no remains of the substantial house, orchards, and gardens remain today, though Nun Street and Nun's Lane are reminders of it. It would have been a centre of culture mainly for the widows and daughters of the wealthy. The well-to-do nuns eventually owned much land in Newcastle and in 1513 leased the Nuns Moor to the town. In 1540 they, like the friaries, were suppressed by Henry VIII and the area they occupied became known as the 'Nuns Field'. Burials of nuns, and other prominent citizens, took place in their church or churchyard. The churchyard was probably situated near the junction of Grainger Street and Newgate Street where human remains have been unearthed during building work.

FRIARS

Orders of friars (meaning brothers, from the French 'frère') arrived in Newcastle during the 13th century. They were penniless, having taken vows of poverty, chastity and obedience, and bridged the huge gap that existed between the rich and poor. Sometimes known as 'salvationists', friars were usually invited and sponsored by local wealthy merchants to live amongst the poor, provide some social and medical services and raise and redistribute money. During the 14th century religious houses – churches, hospitals, friaries and a nunnery, owned a large part of the town and around a quarter of the population were employed in religious activities.

FRANCISCANS (GREY FRIARS)

Followers of St Francis of Assisi, these friars wore grey habits and went barefoot. They arrived in Newcastle in 1237 and settled within the town walls near the Pilgrim Gate about where Pilgrim Street meets Northumberland street today. No buildings survive. They are remembered in the name High Friar Lane. Their burial ground was approximately where Grey's Monument stands today. During the Wars of the Roses in the 15th century the bodies of the Lancastrian ringleaders beheaded at Sandhill were given an 'honourable burial in the consecrated soil' of Grey Friars.

DOMINICANS (BLACK FRIARS)

These friars, followers of St Dominic, arrived from Spain in 1239. They wore black habits and as they wore shoes were also known as the 'shod' friars. They established a house

Blackfriars, mid-19th century.

inside the town walls near the west gate where some remains of their friary can still be seen at Blackfriars. In 1543 Henry VIII sold the friary and the cemetery to Newcastle Corporation. Many burials had been carried out in their church, chapter house and cemetery. In 1829 two bodies were found below Low Friar Street on the site of the cemetery and presumably many other burials still remain.

CARMELITES (WHITE FRIARS)
Expelled from Mount Carmel, they arrived in Newcastle c.1262 to settle eventually in the Orchard Street area. Nothing remains there, but some skeletons were recovered near Forth Street, and reburied in St John's churchyard.

AUGUSTINE OR AUSTIN FRIARS
Disciples of St Augustine, these black-clad friars arrived in the town in 1291. They settled at Manors where the Holy Jesus Hospital roughly covers the site today, and carried out burials either in their church or in the ground 'between the convent and the town wall'. Fragmentary parts of the friary church and its sacristy remain in the late 16th century tower at the rear of the Hospital building.

FRIARS OF THE HOLY TRINITY (TRINITARIANS)
These friars, dedicated to St Michael, dressed in white robes with a red and blue cross, found accommodation at Wall Knoll in 1360 on a site vacated by the Carmelite friars. Nothing remains of their occupation, but a 'quantity of bones' was found there in the early 1820s.

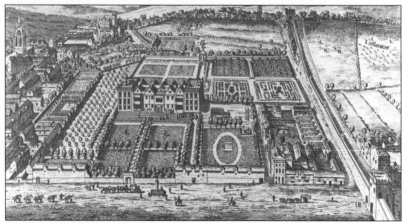

The stately home and grounds of the Blackett family that once stood near the junction of Pilgrim Street and Blackett Street pictured in 1702. Grey Friars occupied the lower right corner of the site near the Pilgrim Gate before the mansion was built. The Nuns' Field lay beyond (upper centre).

THE JEWISH CEMETERY

THORNTON STREET

O n 9th October 1830 seven Jewish residents entered into an agreement to pay various sums of money set down against their names and amounting in all to 4s 9d weekly to form the nucleus of a fund for the purchase of a cemetery and to defray the cost of a wall 'and other expenses attending the said burying ground and wall'.

Initially Jews in Newcastle met for divine worship in a rented room in Pilgrim Street then at various locations including Bigg Market, Pudding Chare, Carliol Street and occasionally in public houses. The site chosen for the cemetery was Thornton Street (off Westgate Road) where, in 1835, 250sq yds of land was purchased at a cost of £62 10s. Shortly afterwards a surrounding wall was built. Today this land is only visible from surrounding buildings and permission is required for access.

In 1838 the first Newcastle Synagogue was built, almost adjoining the cemetery, in a street later known as Temple Street. The stone building measured 60ft sq., cost £360 and included an attached dwelling house for the minister. Extensions took place in 1864. When the building was demolished in 1926 the ornamental stone lintel of the synagogue was moved to Hazelrigg Cemetery.

Rumour persists there was a subterranean passage linking the synagogue with the cemetery; this was probably no more than an enclosed path by the side of the synagogue.

Subsequent Newcastle synagogues followed at Charlotte Square (1867), Leazes Park Road (1879), Corporation Street

West Newcastle Local Studies

The Jewish Cemetery, photographed in 1994.

West Newcastle Local Studies

The building which had been the first Newcastle Synagogue, photographed in 1908, by which time it had become Temple Street Methodist Mission. It was demolished in 1926 and the plaque at the top which reads 'Jews Synagogue: erected Sept XIX: VD XC VIII' was given to the Jewish community.

(1904), Eskdale Terrace (1914) and more recently, Graham Park Road, Gosforth.

The Thornton Street burial ground closed in the early 1850s with interments continuing at Sunderland, the oldest Jewish community in the North East. Only five headstones remain at Thornton Street and are all engraved in Hebrew. In 1857 a site was acquired adjoining the newly opened St John's Parish Cemetery at Elswick, where all the founders of the Jewish community are buried. Twentieth century Jewish cemeteries, still in use, opened at Hazelrigg in 1906 and within the existing Byker and Heaton Cemetery (Benton Road) in 1915.

INDEX OF NAMES

Burdikin, John, soldier 58

Burdon, Richard, publican 60

Burdon-Sanderson, Richard 61

Burn, George, sculptor 139

Cail, Richard, builder 138

Carmichael, J.W., artist 128

Carmichael, Mary, wife of J.W. Carmichael 40

Carr, George Henry, racing cyclist 71

Carr, Humphrey 75

Carr, Nicholas 29

Chaitor, Oswald, linen weaver 30

Chambers, Robert, oarsman 138

Chapman, William, civil engineer 81

Chicken, Edward, poet 34

Clarke, John Graham, coal owner 80

Clarke, Mary 80

Clarke, Mary, mother of Elizabeth Barrett Browning 151

Clasper, Harry, rower 139

Clayton, John, Town Clerk 102

Clayton, Nathaniel, Town Clerk 31

Clennell, Luke, artist 82

Cockburn, Joseph, miner 140

Collingwood, Admiral Lord Cuthbert 17, 19

Conroy, A., pharmacist 116

Cooke, Richard, shipbuilder 144

Cooke, Thomas, businessman 41

Cookson, Isaac, industrialist 18

Cookson, William Isaac, industrialist 104

Cooper, Claude A., showman 134

Corsair, Native American child 118

Coulthard, Thomas, brewer 128

Coutts, John, shipbuilder 144

Cowen, Joseph, politician 87

Crawhall, Joseph, ropemaker 126

Crozer, James, pharmacist (Dirty Dick) 116

Cruddas, George, industrialist 42

Cruddas, W.D., industrialist 42

Cunningham, John, poet 31, 33

Curtis, William Edward, physicist 89

Davenport, James, flax merchant 26

Davidson, John, miller 112

Davidson, Thomas 132

Davidson, William, victim of Great Fire 112

Davy, Sir Humphrey, chemist 152

Dees, John, mason 157

Dent, George 58

Dent, John Moore, printer 114

Dixon, Allan, ropemaker 57

Dixon, John, miner 139

Dobson, John, architect 75, 101

Doubleday, Thomas, poet 100, 153

Dunn, A.M., architect 27

Dunn, Elizabeth 122

Durant, William, preacher 169

Easterby, Anthony, soapmaker 153

Embleton, Dennis, physician 90

Eno, James Crossley, pharmacist 90

Errington, Edward, Town Fool 36

Evetts, L., stained glass artist 144

Eyre, John Lewis, RC priest 123

Faddy, Jane 65

Faraday, Michael, chemist 104, 154

Farnon, John, owner of Farnon's store 159

Fenwick, John 143

Fenwick, John, lawyer 116

Fenwick, Nicholas, merchant adventurer 76

Fletcher, Rev William, RC priest 123

Forbes, John Burghersh, hero of Balaclava 90

Forster, J.R., pharmacist 116

Forster, Thomas, miner 157

Freeman, Paddy, farmer 113

Fukamachi, paymaster in Japanese Navy 43

Gardner, Alexander, footballer 69

Garnett, Joseph, chemist 61

Gascoigne, Joseph, miner 160

Gaskell, Mrs, novelist 84

Gibb, Charles John, surgeon 42

Gibb, Sir Claude Dixon, industrialist 91

Gilchrist, Robert, poet 130

Grainger, Rachel 31

Grainger, Richard, property developer 31, 60, 99, 101, 116

Grassi, Luigi, jeweller 25

Green, Benjamin, architect 66, 99, 116

Green, John, architect 106, 111

Greenfield, Thomas, miner 149

Grey, James, fireman 56

Haggie, Robert Hood, rope manufacturer 113

Hair, Thomas Harrison, artist 72, 157

Haldane, Isabella Mitchelson 61

Hall, John, physician 62

Hall, John, ship owner 91

Hall, William, cutler 75

Hardcastle, William, surgeon 31

Harris, Rev John, missionary 65

Havelock, John 57

Headlam, Thomas Emerson, physician 92

Hedley, Ralph, artist 52, 93, 134

Hedley, Thomas soap maker 154

Hedley, William, yeoman 161

Henderson, George 126

Henderson, Robert of Trinity House 21

Heron, Ralph 21

Herschel, William, astronomer 80

Hicks, W.S., architect 143

Higham, A.B., architect 138

Hill, J.J., architect 120

Hodgson, John, MP 101

Hodgson, Solomon, newspaper proprietor 34

Horsley, Thomas, merchant 21

Hudson, George, 'railway king' 95

Hume, Cardinal Basil 94, 123

Hume, George Haliburton, surgeon 94

Hume, William Errington, physician 94

Hunter, Sir George Burton, shipbuilder 95, 147

I'Anson family 111

I'Anson, William Andrew, surgeon 111

Ingham, William, surgeon 43

Jacobson, Lionel, chairman of Jackson the Tailor 135

James, Daniel, manager of Walker blast furnace 141

James, Thomas, blast furnace builder 141

Johnson, Cuthbert, tobacconist 132

Johnson, R.J. architect 143

Killingworth, John, vicar of St Bartholomew's 143

Lambert, Cuthbert of Lambert's Leap 77

Lambert, Cuthbert, surgeon 77

Larkin, Charles Fox, surgeon 43

Lawson, Dorothy, devoted Roman Catholic 59

Lawson, John, miner 157